Science Notebooks

Writing About Inquiry

Lori Fulton &
Brian Campbell

SECOND EDITION

Foreword by
Rebecca E. Dyasi & Hubert M. Dyasi

HEINEMANN
Portsmouth, NH

Heinemann
361 Hanover Street
Portsmouth, NH 03801–3912
www.heinemann.com

Offices and agents throughout the world

The authors and publisher wish to thank those who have generously given permission to reprint borrowed material:

Figures 2–1, 2–11, 3–5, 3–6, 3–7, 5–2, 5–3, and 6–2 collected, photographed, and reprinted by permission of the Full Option Science System program, Lawrence Hall of Science, University of California, Berkeley. Copyright © 2013, The Regents of the University of California. All rights reserved.

Excerpts and Figure 5–1 from *A Framework for K–12 Science Education: Practices, Crosscutting Concepts, and Core Ideas* by the National Academy of Sciences. Copyright © 2012 by the National Academy of Sciences. Reprinted by permission of The National Academies Press, Washington, DC.

Excerpts from Common Core State Standards © Copyright 2010. National Governors Association Center for Best Practices and Council of Chief State School Officers. All rights reserved.

Library of Congress Cataloging-in-Publication Data
Fulton, Lori.
    Science notebooks : writing about inquiry / Lori Fulton and Brian Campbell ; foreword by Rebecca E. Dyasi, Hubert M. Dyasi. — Second edition.
        pages   cm
    Prev. ed. main entry Campbell, Brian.
    Includes bibliographical references.
    ISBN 978-0-325-05659-3
    1. Science—Study and teaching (Elementary)—United States. 2. School notebooks—United States.
3. Learning by discovery.   I. Campbell, Brian.   II. Campbell, Brian, Science notebooks.   III. Title.

LB1585.3.C36 2014
372.35'044—dc23   2013040600

Editor: Katherine Bryant
Production: Vicki Kasabian
Cover and interior designs: Monica Ann Crigler
Typesetter: Kim Arney
Manufacturing: Steve Bernier

Printed in the United States of America on acid-free paper
18 17   VP   3 4 5

We would like to thank all those students, teachers, and educators who have supported us in our work.

We want to dedicate this book to young scientists everywhere, especially Grace and Savannah. May notebooks serve as tools to help you make sense of the world around you.

Contents

We tried to fiter the material from the water with a screen. Only gravel worked.

Water and earth would not seperate. I guess the fibers are too thin. The salt certainly didn't come out, it had already dissolved.

Going to try filtering with a funnel. Gravel worked again.

Salt worked too & the water was purified and the salt got stuck in the water. Now for earth.

Waiting...   Catherine

Foreword

This book is about the educational power of that constant, venerable, and veritable scientists' companion, the science notebook; but it is also about a lot more. It is about how students can create and use science notebooks both to learn science content and to communicate it effectively. It is also about the respective roles of teachers and of students during inquiry-based science lessons in the elementary school: How students and teachers can interact with one another, individually and jointly assess for learning, and make decisions about further learning. And it is about implementing new science standards and about making links to language arts and literacy.

The authors are experienced elementary school teachers and science education scholars who developed and used science notebooks in their own classrooms. They rightly see the science notebook as the core of an inquiry-based classroom culture characterized by authentic interactions between teacher and students, between students, and between students and their materials and their notebooks, all in pursuit of scientific understanding and explanation.

The authors provide a rich, lucid guide and resource for teachers who want to build that kind of culture. Their book is richly illustrated with lively classroom vignettes showing teachers engaging students in creating and using science notebooks in the context of scientific investigations. These vignettes demonstrate how using science notebooks leads toward the primary goal of science instruction: understanding scientific content. They also illuminate the uniqueness of each student's science notebook as well as elements common to all notebooks (collecting and organizing data, recording questions, and developing explanations, for instance). They describe, for example, how a teacher introduced students to science notebooks through an investigation of water (related to a specific content goal). The process encompasses initial exploration, development of a whole class notebook to serve as a model, and the teacher's orchestration of questions and discussions around collected observations and findings. Fulton and Campbell show how different teachers stimulate students' interest in learning strategies for documenting science practices, core science content, and cross-cutting concepts, and in making meaning of science learning. Students learn to "write purposefully on their understanding" and to "process their thinking."

Throughout the vignettes, the authors give useful practical pointers, such as using learning progressions to be aware of reasonable expectations for students at different stages of development during the year and across grades, making sure students are thinking rather than merely copying from a class notebook, helping students develop ownership of their individual science notebooks; making sure students know how to use their science notebooks as a resource; and not treating science notebook activity as a test.

Science Notebooks is an excellent account of best practice in teaching and learning inquiry-based science at the elementary school level. Its pedagogical approach is firmly rooted in widely recognized research findings about how people learn: It calls for building on the knowledge children bring to school, and for teaching children to engage in scientific reasoning and argument using evidence from their investigations, to use their current conceptual knowledge to build new knowledge, and to continually monitor their own learning. The teacher's roles portrayed in the book are completely in line with the highly acclaimed science teaching standards of the National Science Education Standards and with the Next Generation Science Standards. The authors also show how using science notebooks directly contributes to the development of knowledge and skills described in the Common Core State Standards for English Language Arts: talking, listening, writing, and reading are critical aspects of the science notebook.

Fulton and Campbell devote a chapter to professional scientists and engineers discussing the science (or engineering) notebooks in their professional lives. They make remarkably powerful statements showing how pervasive and pivotal the science notebook is and how true scientific inquiry or engineering design work can be achieved with the use of notebooks. The book's vivid images of the science class invoke parallels with a science or engineering research community in all its attributes of exploration. It demonstrates how to implement authentic science activity in elementary school classrooms.

—Rebecca E. Dyasi
Long Island University, Brooklyn, New York
—Hubert M. Dyasi
Retired Professor of City College and City University of New York

Introduction

What is the purpose of this book?

The main emphasis of this book is to begin teachers on a journey in developing the use of science notebooks in their elementary classrooms. For those already on this journey, the purpose is to aid in the overall development of notebooks. This book is not designed as a step-by-step guide, but as a resource to develop strategies and methods to make notebooks more meaningful.

Who is the audience of this book?

This book is primarily written for elementary classroom teachers using hands-on, inquiry-based science, which allows for more opportunities to utilize the information presented. However, preservice teachers, middle school science and literacy teachers, administrators, literacy specialists, and English language learner facilitators would benefit from various sections as well.

Why a second edition?

Since the first edition was published in 2003, there have been changes to the standards addressing science and literacy. In science, *A Framework for K–12 Science Education* (National Research Council 2012) and the Next Generation Science Standards (Achieve 2013) were published. In literacy, the Common Core State Standards for English Language Arts & Literacy in History/Social Studies, Science, and Technical Subjects (National Governors Association Center for Best Practices, Council of Chief State School Officers 2010) was published in 2010. Science notebooks can play an important role in helping students acquire the ideas, practices, and capacities addressed in all of these documents. These ideas are fully developed in Chapters 5 and 6.

In addition to addressing the new standards, we have added new material to each chapter. In Chapter 1, strategies to support or scaffold science notebook instruction have been added. In Chapters 2, 3, and 5, we examine the role science notebooks play in the development of explanations and arguments. In Chapter 3, we have also added strategies for collecting and analyzing science notebooks for formative purposes. We've added new interviews with a scientist and two engineers to Chapter 4, and we've brought in more than twenty new pieces of student work throughout the book.

What are science notebooks?

Science notebooks are a natural complement to kit-based programs in which students are actively engaged with materials, involved in small- and whole-group discussions, and using expository text as a reference to confirm or extend ideas after investigations. In the elementary school classroom, science notebooks are a record of students' findings, questions, thoughts, procedures, data, explanations, and wonderings that may or may not retell the journey of their science experience.

Science notebooks are

- tools for students to use during science;
- tattered—a sign of regular use—with water stains and bent corners;
- always near children, tucked under their arms or close at hand, so they can record a moment in time as they work with the materials;
- personal to the owners and might make sense only to them;
- places to record data, observations, illustrations, understandings, questions, reflections, and ideas while working;
- reference tools students use as they continue their work or talk with others in small- or whole-group discussions.

What can be used as a science notebook?

- a composition book
- a spiral notebook
- a three-ring binder
- a three-prong paper folder
- folded paper

What is the difference among science journals, logs, and notebooks?

As science notebooks gain in popularity, more and more people are using some sort of recording device in their classrooms. Teachers often refer to them as *science journals* or *logs*, as well as *notebooks*. Although teachers may use these words interchangeably, the differences among them have led many people to question how others are using these recording devices.

Being familiar with journals in other subject areas, some teachers ask their students to keep journals in science as well. Journals often serve as reflections of students' learning. In science, journals are kept in the desk during the investigation and used only after the work is done and the materials are put away. Most entries usually begin with "Today in science I. . . ." In this sense, journals contain reflections of students' work and not necessarily the data from their investigations.

When teachers refer to *logs*, they often mean books where students keep data over time. In science, logs are used during investigations but are not used during discussions. Students might look back at the data but do not reflect on their understandings or synthesize the data within the log itself.

Notebooks are meant to be tools for students to record both their data and thinking as they work with materials. Students use them prior to the investigation to record their thinking or planning; during the investigation to record words, pictures, photos, or numbers, possibly getting the notebooks wet and messy in the process; and after the investigation to help clarify their thinking and data to share them with others.

Science notebooks are more than a collection of notes about science. Science notebooks replicate, to a certain degree, the notebooks that scientists keep. They contain plans, questions, quantitative and qualitative data, thoughts, explanations, analysis, and more. The development of content through scientific practices drives the science notebook for students. Language strategies support the content development; for example, the teacher might use a Venn diagram as a way to help students compare and contrast the structures of two different organisms. The teacher facilitates the use of the skills of comparing and contrasting within the science notebook as a way to develop a better conceptual understanding of structures of organisms.

We use the general term *scientific practices* to refer to the work of both scientists and engineers throughout this book.

What are the goals of a science notebook?

There are three goals for using science notebooks with students. The primary goal is to build and reveal students' thinking about science content. Whether in a school focused on meeting the Next Generation Science Standards or in an informal after-school setting, students should be thinking deeply about science content as they use their science notebooks. The notebook serves as a space for students to communicate that thinking. The second goal of notebooks is to replicate the work of scientists. Scientists plan investigations, collect data, interpret those data, and construct explanations as they work. They document this work in their science notebooks and report their findings to the scientific community. Their notebooks are an important tool in their work. The last goal is to serve as a tool to develop and exercise literacy skills. The science notebook provides a vehicle in which students write and organize information and thoughts. The notebook is used as a resource when speaking to their peers and as a reference to be read to access prior experiences and connect thinking across months of work.

What is in this book?

This book is designed as a reference for the classroom teacher. The first three chapters focus on classroom implementation, and the last three chapters provide rationale for using notebooks. These sections should be read as needed to help teachers meet their goals in developing science notebooks in the classroom. Within certain sections are vignettes (short stories). These vignettes are based upon the authors' experiences when working with children in a variety of settings utilizing science notebooks. Thinking points are presented throughout the chapters and are designed to help link the ideas presented in this book to the classroom and philosophical beliefs. The thinking points should be revisited from time to time as your thinking changes as you gain experience with notebooks.

What does the teacher do?

Chapter 1 focuses on the role of the teacher in implementing science notebooks, sharing ideas of how to establish goals for notebook use, getting authentic notebooks started, and developing them further without infringing upon the notebook's authenticity. The chapter also examines ways to purposefully use strategies to develop notebooks to help all children, including English language learners.

What is in a science notebook?

Chapter 2 explores the elements of science notebooks and closely examines what notebooks might look like. We share some ideas for helping students record and organize their data using both words and drawings, and we examine the importance of questioning. The chapter also explores how to take students beyond simply recording data to developing explanations containing claims, evidence, and reasoning, as well as synthesizing their thoughts before, during, and after an investigation.

What are signs of students' progress?

Chapter 3 examines how students progress as they utilize science notebooks. It opens by considering the role of formative assessment and ways in which teachers can collect information on student progress. Next, the chapter shifts to how students progress from beginning to more advanced stages in their representation related to the scientific practices as well as their conceptual understandings.

What does the scientific community have to say about science notebooks?

Chapter 4 shares conversations with scientists and engineers. Because notebooks are an important component of the scientific world, this chapter discusses what scientists consider to be important elements of a notebook and examines how scientists use notebooks in their line of work.

How do notebooks support implementation of the Next Generation Science Standards?

Chapter 5 examines how notebooks can foster the development of scientific practices, crosscutting concepts, and core ideas and discusses the implications on students' learning. Connections to the Next Generation Science Standards are shared.

How do science notebooks promote literacy development?

Chapter 6 discusses the use of science notebooks as a context for literacy development, looking at connections between science notebooks and the development of speaking and listening, reading, writing, and the use of vocabulary as identified in the Common Core State Standards for English Language Arts.

The Role of the Teacher

As with any practice within the classroom, the teacher's role is crucial to success with science notebooks. Getting students to use science notebooks to their fullest extent allows students to develop and reveal their thinking about scientific concepts, replicate the work of scientists and engineers, and develop and exercise language skills. The teacher needs to carefully plan how to manage time, materials, and students as notebooks are used and to consider carefully the type of notebook used, what is recorded, and what tools and strategies benefit students' content and language development.

Planning

Where to begin?

There are certain decisions to make before beginning to use science notebooks in the classroom. Grade level and student ability should be considered in these decisions, as they factor into initial student use of the science notebook. These decisions include such things as:

- What type of notebook should be used?
- What should be included with every notebook entry?
- What will students write about in their notebooks?
- What organizational tools will students need?
- What role will students' language abilities play?
- Which experience will provide students with a meaningful starting point?

What type of notebook should be used?

To begin, the teacher must decide the physical structure of the science notebook. There are a variety of options, including composition books, spiral notebooks, three-ring binders, two-pocket folders with prongs, or pieces of folded paper stapled with or without a cover. Preference on the type of notebook varies; however, many have found the composition book allows students to keep a running record of the work and thinking they do throughout the year and represents growth over time. Using a composition book provides ample flexibility for first-time use. If using instructional materials that will require students to glue or tape sheets into their notebooks, the notebook should be large enough so students have ample room to attach those sheets. Samples that appear in this book come from students who used composition books.

THINKING POINT: What type of notebook will you use?

What should be included with every notebook entry?

Another decision the teacher must consider is what information will be recorded within each entry. Scientists often record the date, time, and weather. These items might not seem important in elementary science; however, by including this information in every entry, students are establishing habits of scientific documentation. Younger students can start with a date initially and add additional information as they are able. Many teachers find it helpful for themselves and their students to include a subject or title with each entry. This becomes a quick reference to locate information as students flip through their notebooks during discussion.

THINKING POINT: What information will you expect students to include in all entries?

What will students write about in their notebooks?

Chapter 2, "Elements of a Science Notebook," offers a variety of ideas for recording.

Notebooks provide a medium in which students document scientific investigations. Students will approach the process of documentation from different perspectives and the teacher should take this into consideration. For example, it might be more realistic to initially expect drawings from first graders than the use of Venn diagrams.

It takes time before students begin to use many of the elements of a notebook, so it is important to have reasonable expectations. Beginning entries might appear discouraging, but from there you can determine where students are starting and how much scaffolding might be needed. Some entries will contain only observations and others will offer interpretations or inferences of those observations. Some students might draw smiley faces on animals and write that their insect likes them. This should be expected, as students are most familiar and comfortable with that form of writing and drawing. Students will progress as they continue to work with notebooks and use them in their discussions with others. The more students use their notebooks, the more scientific their representations become. Students develop at different rates and their notebooks are no exception. Some students take to their notebooks right away, recording in great detail, while other students require extensive scaffolding to become proficient. Figures 1–1 and 1–2 show beginning entries from students at two different grade levels. What do you notice about these two entries?

Chapter 3 describes how students progress and how teachers can use formative assessment to guide this development.

THINKING POINT: **What are realistic expectations for your students' writing?**

What organizational tools will students need?

In the beginning you will need to talk with students about the overall organization of their notebooks. One technique that might help with organization is the use of colored tabs. For example, a red tab could mark the section on organisms and a yellow tab might signify the solids and liquids section. It might also be helpful to talk with students about using the next blank page rather than skipping around in their notebooks or using an entire page to record information rather than putting only one piece of information on a page. Although these might sound like simple ideas, some students struggle with organizational skills, and such techniques might require direction in the form of guiding questions, minilessons, or modeling from both teachers and students.

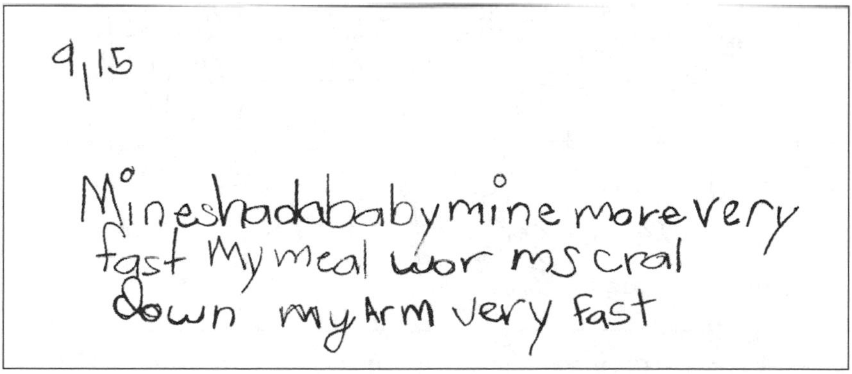
9,15

Mineshadababymine more very fast My meal wor ms cral down my Arm very fast

Figure 1–1. Beginning notebook entry of a second grader describing how fast a mealworm crawls

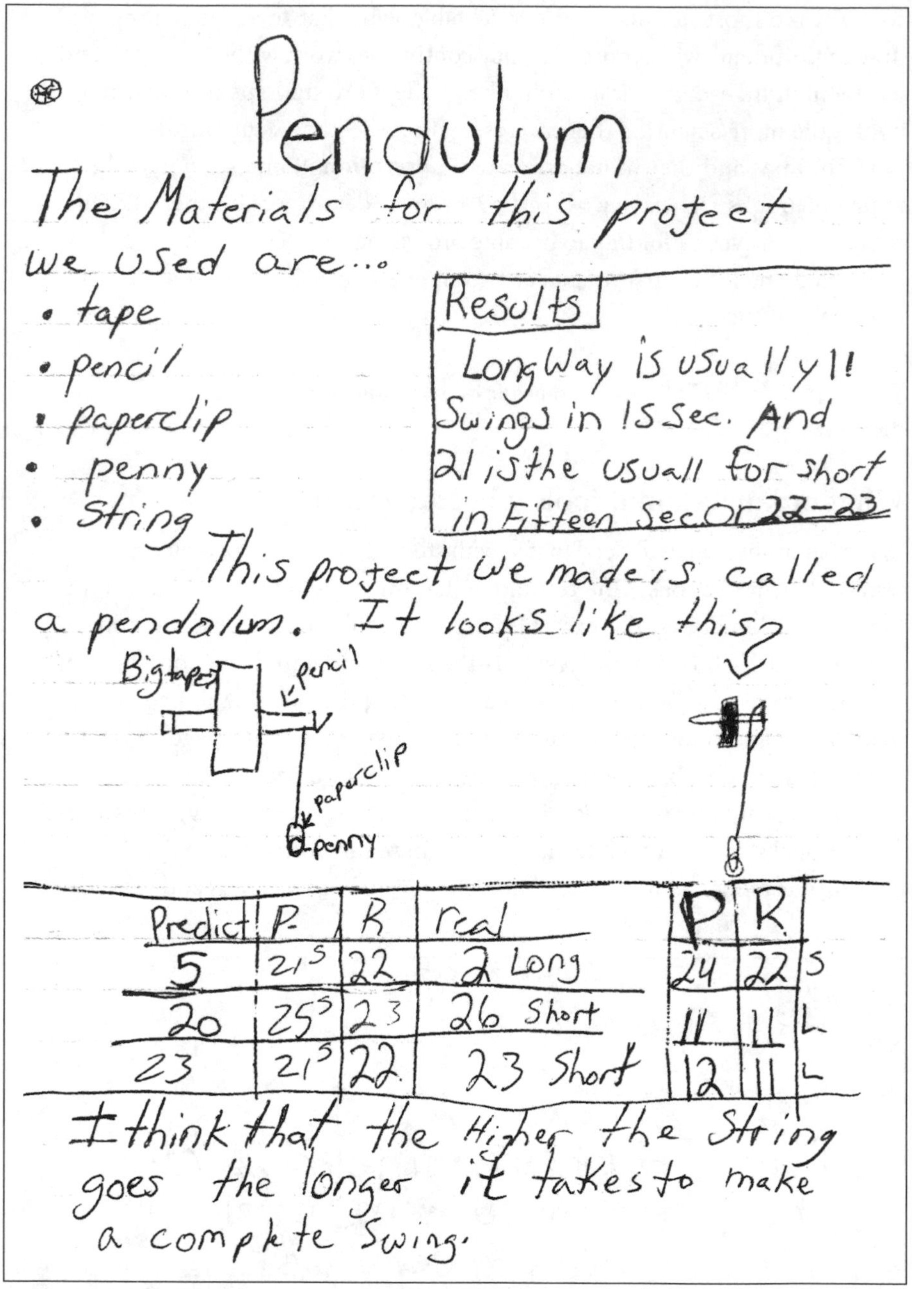

Pendulum

The Materials for this project
we used are...
- tape
- pencil
- paperclip
- penny
- string

Results

LongWay is usually II!
Swings in 15 Sec. And
21 is the usuall for short
in Fifteen Sec. Or 22-23

This project we made is called
a pendolum. It looks like this?

Big tape   pencil

paperclip
penny

Predict	P-	R	real		P	R.	
5	21.5	22	2 Long		24	22	S
20	25.5	23	26 Short		11	11	L
23	21.5	22	23 Short		12	11	L

I think that the Higher the String
goes the longer it takes to make
a complete swing.

Figure 1–2. Beginning notebook entry of a fifth grader

The teacher's own organizational habits, whether they be sequential or random, often impact the outcome of students' notebooks. A word of caution about teaching only one style of organization: some students might have a difficult time following a certain line of thinking, causing frustration for both students and teacher. Yet it is important to establish some sense of organization initially; notebooks that are too random might not be useful tools. Providing too much structure will also limit the ability to determine what students are able to do independently. By allowing students choice in their organization, such as where they put the date or whether they use a drawing or words to capture their thinking, the teacher is helping them build an important skill. In time and with feedback and appropriate guidance, students will find an organizational technique that works for them.

THINKING POINT: What organizational tools do your students need?

What role will students' language abilities play in notebook development?

Teachers with young students or students who have limited experiences with English will need to consider what additional scaffolding and strategies might be needed to support science notebook development. Some might be surprised to find that even their articulate students have limited experience with the language of science, as the procedural and conceptual language of science is often new to all students. There is usually a range of language abilities within the classroom, and different scaffolds and strategies are effective for different students. Some teachers prefer to provide a high level of support initially and modify the strategies as the year progresses. Other teachers start with a moderate amount of support and then modify. Both approaches have benefits and limitations. With more support, the students might feel more successful, but it is difficult to determine what students can do independently. Alternatively, with less support, students might struggle more initially but the teacher can better gauge what students are able to do independently. Specific strategies for scaffolding are shared later in this chapter.

THINKING POINT: How will you support students' language needs and development?

What experience will provide students with a meaningful starting point?

One of the most important things to consider in the beginning is what kind of investigation will provide a solid foundation for the development of good scientific practices and appropriate content. Students in younger grades have fewer experiences with scientific practices than older students and will need guidance on how to make observations or follow procedures. The first experience should offer students the opportunity to record using various techniques. Observations that require more than one sense often work well. Having students observe familiar materials, such as the properties of a specific fruit or leaf or a section of the school grounds, would serve as an appropriate beginning activity. Because this investigation will set the stage for future recordings, it is important that it is engaging, promotes scientific conversation, and is developmentally appropriate.

THINKING POINT: What will you use as your initial investigation?

After considering ideas on

- the type of notebook,
- information to be included in all entries,
- realistic expectations,
- organizational tools,
- language abilities, and
- the initial investigation,

the teacher is ready to implement science notebooks.

Initial Implementation of Science Notebooks

After considering all these initial issues, the next step is to implement notebooks in the classroom. As you begin to put notebooks into practice, there are new considerations:

- What goals will science notebooks address?
- What will the first week actually look like?

What goals will science notebooks address?

One element of teaching involves setting goals for students' learning. When using science notebooks, teachers need to thoughtfully plan specific goals related to

1. content,
2. scientific practices and crosscutting concepts, and
3. language and communication skills.

The first goal focuses on building scientific concepts. Students use their science notebooks to record their findings and ideas about a content goal, such as the effects of environmental changes on organisms. Such goals come from national and state standards and are addressed in quality science curricula that not only identify these content goals but also sequence them in a logical progression to build toward understanding core ideas in science. The content goal may lead to a focus question meant to guide the instruction and reveal students' understanding of the content, such as "How does an increase in rain affect plant life?" Students communicate their thinking as they answer this question in their notebooks. (The focus of this book is on using science notebooks as learning tools to develop these ideas rather than the development and selection of such content goals or focus questions.)

The second goal emphasizes the advancement of scientific practices and crosscutting concepts, such as analyzing and interpreting data and determining patterns. The science notebook provides an authentic means for students to engage with these practices and concepts in much the same way that scientists engage with them.

Finally, the third goal focuses on the development of students' language and communication skills, such as supporting claims with evidence. The science notebook provides students with a venue to develop these skills in a meaningful context related to their firsthand experiences.

With clear learning goals in mind, it is easier for the teacher to facilitate students' experiences with science notebooks and guide students toward the desired understandings. Begin by looking at the identified content goals within the curriculum you use. For example, a curriculum might suggest "Water can change the shape of the land" as a content goal. This content factors into instructional decisions for the science notebook. (If your curriculum does not provide these stated goals, it will be up to you to determine them based on your standards and required topics.) As students work toward this content goal within their notebooks, you might notice that students need to further develop their observation skills and plan to focus on a goal related to that scientific practice by modeling a technical drawing to address the skill. Later, you might introduce sentence frames to scaffold students' explanations about the ways in which water can change the shape of the land, supporting a goal related to students' ability to communicate a scientific explanation.

As you read the following vignette (from a second-grade classroom after a few months of using science notebooks), notice the goals the teacher is setting for the students.

> At the beginning of each investigation, I looked at what the students would be doing and considered: (1) What were the content goals for this activity? For example, were students investigating the physical characteristics of an insect or determining what affected the pitch of an instrument? (2) What were the main scientific practices being used? For example, were students obtaining, communicating, or evaluating information? In most science activities, there were several scientific practices occurring over time and it was difficult to focus on all of them; however, I tried to select one on which to focus. (3) What different ways did students represent information? Because I consider notebooks to be tools for the students, I focused on different ways the students recorded the information, not necessarily the way I would do it. In addition, I also considered what language supports my students might need to help them effectively represent their ideas. For example, I made sure vocabulary was easily accessible for students to use as they wrote. Once I determined the focus of the lesson in terms of content, practice, and representation, I was able to focus on facilitating the interactions between the students and their notebooks.

In this vignette, the teacher established three goals—a content goal, a scientific practice goal, and a goal on how to communicate that information in the notebook.

As with any good teaching, the goals of the lesson will shift over time according to students' needs and teacher comfort level. In the beginning, notebook instruction might only focus on a single content goal, a scientific practice, or language skills. As the year progresses, the teacher begins to focus on multiple goals including a goal for content, a goal for particular scientific practices or concepts, and a third goal on the use of language within the notebook.

What will the first week actually look like?

Because science notebooks might be new to students, it is important to thoroughly plan the first few days of use. A thorough plan allows you to think through all aspects and prepare for the unexpected. Although the scientific concept might differ from lesson to lesson, the process of learning to use notebooks is quite similar in all lessons. In the following example, the teacher begins by having students observe apples to provide a common experience with a familiar material. This allows students to focus on their notebooks and develop observation skills. The teacher can also choose to focus more on specific concepts, such as variation of the apples or structure and function of parts of the apple, during the discussion. After the initial introductory lesson, the teacher introduces new materials that students will study more in depth, developing additional skill as well as content. Since these lessons address both science and language, they could take place during both science and language arts instructional time.

DAY ONE

Objective: Students will record observations of an apple.

Materials: apples, hand lenses, notebooks

Procedure (50+ minutes):

1. Introduce the lesson: discuss with students that they will be observing an apple and recording what they notice. (2 minutes)
2. Introduce notebooks as tools to help students keep track of their observations. Discuss the essential components of every entry (date and subject) with students. (5 minutes)
3. Have students observe the apple and record their findings. (10 minutes)

4. Ask students to sit in a circle on the floor and share recorded observations of their apple with a partner. (3 minutes)

5. Ask students to share observations as a whole group using their science notebooks. Record observations on the board. (10 minutes)

6. Have students share how they recorded their information (words, sentences, pictures). Ask students to discuss the benefits of various recording methods. (5 minutes)

7. Introduce the hand lens and how to use it. (2 minutes)

8. Pose a question, such as "What do apples look like?" (grades K–2) or "How do apples vary in appearance?" (grades 3–5). Have students record the question in their notebook and provide time for students to partner with another student to continue observing their apples, making comparisons and adding to their recordings. (10 minutes)

9. Have students return to the floor and share their observations with each other, focusing on the similarities and differences in their apples. (3 minutes)

10. Return to the question posed earlier. Have students discuss their thinking with a new partner and record their answer in their notebook. Provide a sentence starter, such as "Some apples have. . . ." (grades K–2) or "Some ways apples are different from each other are. . . ." (grades 3–5). (5–10 minutes)

DAY TWO

Objective: Students will record observations of plant structures. Patterns of discussion will be established.

Materials: plants, notebooks

Procedure (50 minutes):

1. Gather students on the floor to read the responses to the question they recorded on day one. Invite students to share their observations with the whole group by asking questions about the color and shape of the apples. Ask students to provide their evidence if applicable. (5 minutes)

2. Ask students to look at how they recorded the information in their notebooks. Have students discuss how the method they used to record was effective. (5 minutes)

3. Introduce the plant(s): share with students that they will work with partners to observe and record information about their plant. Ask

students, "What can you observe about your plant?" to guide their entries. (15 minutes)

4. Have students return to the floor and share their findings with a different partner. (5 minutes)
5. Ask students to share their observations with the whole group. After one student shares his observations, provide time for other students to ask questions or make comments regarding what was shared. (10 minutes)
6. After the discussion, give students time to record any additional information they would like to add to their notebooks. (5 minutes)
7. Have students return to the plants to make further observations. (5 minutes)

DAY THREE

Objective: Students will record observations of plant structures. Students will be introduced to relevant vocabulary. Students will discuss methods of recording.

Materials: plants, hand lenses, notebooks

Procedure (45+ minutes):

1. Ask students to sit on the floor and individually review their notebook entries from the previous day prior to discussing their observations with a new partner. (5 minutes)
2. Have individuals share observations with the whole group. Continue to provide time for questions and comments for each student. (5 minutes)
3. Discuss with students that they will be looking at the same plants as before, but this time a hand lens will be available. (2 minutes)

> By providing a hand lens, students can discuss the scale of their drawings when recording their observations.

4. Prior to returning to the plants, ask students to think about what they are going to observe. Allow time for students to discuss ideas with others. Once they have a focus in mind, ask the students how they plan to record their observations. Have students share how they are going to record (pictures, labels, sentences, etc.). (5 minutes)
5. Have students return to the plants and make further observations. (15 minutes)
6. Ask students to return to the floor and share observations. As students share their observations, listen for the terminology they use to describe the plant structures. Connect students' informal language to formal vocabulary, such as *stems* or *veins*. (10 minutes)

> These words can be added to the word wall after being introduced.

7. Prior to cleaning up, provide students with time to add to their observations. Students might or might not naturally incorporate new words that were introduced during the discussion. Encourage students to use the words if they find them helpful in describing their observations. (3 minutes)

DAY FOUR

Objective: Students will draw and label plant structures.

Materials: plants, hand lenses, notebooks, colored pencils

Procedure (52 minutes):

1. Gather students on the floor and review their recordings from the previous days. (2 minutes)
2. In groups of three or four, ask students to discuss different ways they recorded their information. As students share out, ask them to explain how they recorded their information. (5 minutes)
3. After all groups have shared how they recorded their information, focus on drawings of the plants. Discuss what information might be shown in a drawing. Guide students to notice that the plant structures can be recorded quite easily using a drawing. Ask students what else might help them record plant structures along with the drawings. Guide students to use labels along with their drawings to show the various parts of the plant. Older students might suggest different techniques to represent observations made using the hand lens. (10 minutes)
4. Before students continue with their observations, have them discuss with a partner what they might draw and label while observing their plants. (2 minutes)
5. Introduce the colored pencils as tools that they may use to more accurately record their plant observations. (2 minutes)
6. Ask students to observe their plants and record their observations. (15 minutes)
7. Have students return to the floor and share their observations with a different partner. (5 minutes)
8. Focus the whole-group discussion on how observations were recorded. Are students drawing their plants and labeling the structures? Have students share their techniques for recording with the class. (6 minutes)

9. Have students discuss with a partner how they might improve their recording the next time they look at plants. They might need some suggestions, such as using correct colors, labeling the structures, or labeling only the important things rather than everything. (5 minutes)

DAY FIVE

Objective: Students will compare and contrast different plants and variation of structures. Students will develop strategies to record information on two different objects.

Materials: colored pencils, hand lenses, notebooks, different plants

Procedure (60 minutes):

1. Have students review their previous observations. Revisit how students might improve their recording. (5 minutes)
2. Introduce the new plant. Discuss with the students that they will be looking at a new type of plant today. Students might wish to revisit the first plant to compare it with the new plant. Have students think about how they are going to record the information on their new plant. Have a few students share their recording strategies. (10 minutes)
3. Have students observe and record information about their new plant with a partner. Students might revisit the first plant and add information to their notebooks. (10 minutes)
4. Gather students on the floor to share their findings with each other. (3 minutes)
5. Ask students to share their findings with the whole group. Students will need to clarify which plant they are discussing. (10 minutes)
6. After the students have shared, have them look at their notebooks and discuss how they might organize the information about the two separate plants to see how they are similar and different. Share strategies with the whole group. (5 minutes)
7. Before returning to their plants, have students think about how they will organize their information. Let them know that it is okay to try new ways to find one that works best for them. (2 minutes)
8. Have students return to their plants to make more observations and organize their information to make it easier to determine how the two plants are similar and different. (10 minutes)

9. Ask students to return to the floor. Pose the question, "How do plant structures vary?" Have students discuss their thinking and provide evidence to support their thinking. Students can record their thinking using a sentence frame, such as "I think . . . because. . . ." (5 minutes)

This schedule is one way to introduce science notebooks. Teachers might make adjustments to accommodate student readiness. As in any subject area, the teacher needs to constantly assess where students are and adjust the plan accordingly. The next section looks more closely at the role science notebooks play in informing instructional practice.

Formative Assessment

An assessment functions formatively to the extent that evidence about student achievement is elicited, interpreted, and used by teachers, learners, or their peers to make decisions about the next steps in instruction that are likely to be better, or better founded, than the decisions they would have made in the absence of that evidence. (Wiliam 2011, 43)

What role do science notebooks play in formative assessment?

As students use their notebooks, the notebooks become formative assessment tools for both the teacher and the students, serving as an aid in terms of making learning decisions. They are not used by the teacher for summative assessment, nor are they a graded product. Rather, notebooks are tools for informing the teacher if students are meeting predetermined goals or if more instruction needs to be given. Even in the beginning stages of notebook use, it is important to consider students' progress. Following are some questions you might ask regarding students' science notebooks. These might be helpful in determining where students are and what next steps might be appropriate. Other sections of this book provide further information on next steps using the information gathered.

- Do students' drawings enhance their entries?
- How often are students using drawings and how much time are they spending on them?

- How comfortable are students in using labels with their drawings?
- How do labels enhance or detract from the drawings students create?
- Is the use of color enhancing or impeding the students' drawings?
- What types of questions are students asking and recording in their notebooks?
- How much of the students' recording is fact and how much is fiction?
- What types of recording strategies are students using?
- What organizational strategies would make notebooks more useful for students?
- When observing live organisms, how do students represent the behaviors and structures of the organisms?
- What evidence do students show of their thinking and understanding?
- To what extent are students providing evidence and reasoning when answering questions?
- How do students make use of their notebooks in small- and whole-group discussions?
- When do students choose to record information in their notebooks?
- When do students choose to use information in their notebooks?

These questions serve as an initial guide for teachers in determining future goals related to scientific practices or language, such as focusing on students providing evidence to support claims or on students communicating information from their notebooks to their peers.

THINKING POINT: How will I gather data to formatively assess my students?

Developing Science Notebooks

How can student use of the notebook be supported?

One of your most important roles is to support and scaffold students' use of notebooks. To be used in a scientific manner, notebooks need to be available during an investigation and then used in discussions with others. This does not occur naturally for many students and requires assistance from the teacher to become habit. In the beginning, it might seem as though a great deal of time is being invested; consider it as time spent building a solid foundation for scientific thinking.

As students develop science content, they work through several experiences with the materials, notebooks, and class discussions. The following section introduces a general process called the "Cycle of Notebook Interaction." The cycle describes the roles of the students and the teacher throughout an investigation. It is important to note that this cycle might take place over the course of several days. Depending on the goals of the lesson, aspects of the cycle might be in a different order as well. The vignettes throughout the following sections describe how a teacher worked with a fourth-grade class throughout the cycle.

- Materials: Exploration
- Discussion: Setting the Stage
- Materials: Recording Strategies
- Discussion: Recording Strategies
- Materials: Content
- Discussion: Content
- Notebooks: Content and Reflection

MATERIALS: EXPLORATION Whenever students are introduced to something new, it is important that they have time to explore the materials and concepts freely. This allows them to formulate ideas related to the content goal and is very beneficial for students with limited experiences. A general question or challenge can be posed to the students to guide this exploration, such as "What are the properties of these liquids?" or "How can these materials make a system to launch a ball?" Students might or might not record during this initial exploration—that is okay.

DISCUSSION: SETTING THE STAGE This second phase of the cycle takes place only after students have manipulated the materials and allows students to share initial ideas about the content goal, accessing prior knowledge and experiences. The teacher might collect some of the students' initial ideas in a class notebook, planning to revisit these ideas later in the cycle. Additionally, this discussion and the use of the class notebook provides students with the support or scaffolds they might need for documenting scientific practices, such as writing a procedure, asking questions, or collecting data. During this discussion, focus first on setting the stage for the content goal and, if applicable, second on documentation of the scientific practice goal. Exactly how much time for each varies depending on the goals and the students.

Many times throughout the investigation I gathered the students to a discussion area (an area away from their work space where we could go over directions and discuss the activity). I revisited the question I posed earlier, "What do you notice about the way water flows?" They began by sharing their thoughts with someone sitting near them before sharing with the group; this provided everyone the opportunity to share something in a nonthreatening environment. It also allowed students who might not have an idea or be able to verbalize their idea clearly to receive help from others. A few students shared their thinking about the way water flows with the whole group. I did not confirm or reject any ideas at this point, but I took mental note of points to revisit later. I shifted the discussion to get students thinking about how they might record the information. I asked leading questions. For example, "How might you organize the information you are collecting about the way water flows?" We shared our thoughts about recording as a class, and then I asked the group for questions they had about the recording strategies the students shared. Before ending the discussion, I asked students to talk with a partner about what recording strategy they planned to use when they returned to the materials.

After this type of discussion, students have developed initial ideas about the content and discussed a variety of strategies they can use to record their observations and thinking. This provides a level of support for students and focuses their learning for the investigation.

MATERIALS: RECORDING STRATEGIES Once students are focused on how to record, they return to the materials. Although this exploration looks similar to the initial one, there are differences. This time, the teacher collects some data to formatively assess students' thinking about the content goal and their progress on the scientific practice goal. Although these data are collected informally, they can help the teacher determine the focus of the next discussion.

> I frequently walked around during the activity to observe students' communication about the flow of water, the content goal, and their progress on recording their observations, the scientific practice goal. I only interacted with the students to clarify directions or redirect their attention to the activity. They needed this time with the materials to continue formulating their ideas; if I jumped in too quickly, it would likely interrupt their learning. Students needed time to work uninterrupted to develop their thought processes and questions, allowing them to truly internalize the science concepts. During this time, I noted if students were struggling with organizing the data or labeling.

In this vignette, the attention of the teacher is focused on collecting formative assessment data on students' representations in the notebook. The purpose is to allow the teacher to make instructional decisions based on one of the goals for the lesson, in this case, the recording of observations. Depending on the data, the teacher might use these data during the next discussion to guide students or might plan to meet with a small group later.

DISCUSSION: RECORDING STRATEGIES This discussion period becomes a pivotal point in students' recording. Based on data gathered during the last interaction with the materials and the recording strategies used, the teacher chooses a focus for discussion. This discussion can focus on the documentation of a scientific practice (discussed more in Chapter 2), such as technical drawing or building explanations. Through careful questioning, the teacher guides the students to develop various techniques related to the scientific practice goal.

> After a brief fifteen- to twenty-minute period working with the materials, I called the students back for a discussion using their notebooks. I began by asking students what type of recording strategy they used, such as drawings or

tables. Then I asked them to focus on one particular aspect of the investigation, directing their discussion toward how they recorded observations of how water flows. I gave them a couple of minutes to look over their notes and make additions before they shared their thoughts. I asked them to discuss with a friend, using their notebooks, what they observed, how they recorded their observations, and what questions they still had. Then I asked the students to share as a class, again allowing the students time to question each other.

I never skipped sharing with a friend because that is a powerful part of the activity. Sharing is valuable for students because they are working, making progress, and sharing that progress with each other. It holds everyone in the class accountable to each other, as speaking and listening are part of our language arts skills.

Occasionally, if there was a recording convention that was difficult, such as a complex table, I provided some guidance. I modeled this convention in the class notebook and used a think-aloud so students gained insight on when and how to use the new strategy. I intentionally put off most of the content discussion until students had more time with the materials. The last thing we talked about before returning to the investigation was next steps the students would take as they continued to record in their notebooks. Again, the students discussed their next steps with each other before sharing as a class.

In this vignette, the teacher focuses the students' attention on documenting the observations that relate to the content goal, how water flows. A thorough record of their observations is necessary for students to determine the patterns in the data in order to better understand the content. Additionally, this is an opportunity for the teacher to provide some support for the students through a minilesson, peer modeling, or other instructional strategy.

MATERIALS: CONTENT Once students have started to use strategies for recording information, the focus is now on understanding of the content goal.

As students continue to work with the materials, the teacher assesses their understanding and determines next steps to take in terms of the content goal.

> When students returned to the investigation, I observed how they were recording, but this time I was more focused on the content. I interacted more with the students and asked them questions, such as "What are you finding? What are your thoughts? What evidence do you have to support your thinking?" Sometimes I asked why they were recording the information the way they were. I determined how the whole class was progressing. Did they need more time with this experience or did they need more experiences to understand the content?

The teacher encourages informal discussion of the content and recording of those inferences, reasons, and observations within the notebook. These records serve as a precursor to the formal discussion of the content.

DISCUSSION: CONTENT The primary goal of science notebooks is to serve as tools to aid students in building and representing scientific content. Once students have had experience with the concept and have formulated initial ideas, small- and whole-group discussions take place to help students solidify conceptual understandings. The teacher poses questions to help students analyze and interpret data to extract meaning from those data recorded in their notebooks. The focus question is revisited and students discuss their thinking with their peers.

> After students had time to focus on the content, I called them back to the floor. I provided a few minutes for them to write down any thoughts they had not yet recorded, and then I asked them to share with a partner. The purpose of this discussion was to communicate their thinking. Keeping this in mind, I often began the group discussion with a question, such as "What did you discover?" Again, the students discussed this with each other before sharing ideas with the whole group. I asked follow-up questions, such as

"Look at the observations you recorded in your notebook; what patterns do you notice about how water flows?" and "What evidence do you have to support your claim?" This discussion served as an opportunity for students to examine the purpose of their work as well as build speaking and listening skills.

In this vignette, the teacher guides the discussion to build understanding of the content goal. The questions ask students to refer to the information recorded in their notebooks to determine patterns or cause and effect. The notebook is a very valuable tool in this discussion as the teacher prompts for specific pieces of evidence. Additionally, the teacher might ask students to engage in argumentation during this discussion time to deepen or clarify the content. In the vignette above, the teacher could have made the claim "Water flows to the side" or "Water flows when there is a path," providing evidence to support the claim, to encourage students to provide counterclaims supported by evidence from their notebooks.

NOTEBOOKS: CONTENT AND REFLECTION Students benefit from writing in science, as it allows them a means to process their thinking. Generally, this is when students respond to the focus question and write claims or explanations as independently as possible. By giving them time to write purposefully on their understanding of the science concept, the teacher is asking them to make sense of their learning. The teacher can scaffold this communication by providing a language frame for students; however, it is important to ensure that the students are doing the thinking about the content rather than copying from the class notebook or board, as such written communication can serve as a window into their true understanding.

As discussed in Chapter 3, this writing serves as a valuable formative assessment.

I asked students to answer the focus question, "How does water flow?" in their notebooks. I provided a frame for making an explanation of "I think . . . because I observed . . . I think this happens because. . . ." (see Figure 1–3). As students finished recording, I walked around the room and encouraged them to record any additional thoughts or questions that might help them later. I have found that the students who were actively engaged with the materials benefit from this time; it allows them time to process their thoughts without distraction. There were times when we were at the end of the day and students would be so engaged in recording their thoughts that they stayed after the bell rang.

> Water f low's because of it being a Liquid if it was solid. I observed it if it was a solid it would not be Flowing. This also happens by gravity. Gravity, is a big part of helping water flow. Water always flows down, because of gravity.

Figure 1–3. An example of a student explanation using provided sentence frames

This vignette examined what happened after the content discussion, as the focus shifted to the language goal, which was for students to provide reasons supported by evidence. Other language goals, such as making an oral presentation on a topic, might happen after the Cycle of Notebook Interaction during a language arts time using the science notebook as a resource.

By allowing students time to work without interruption on writing an explanation, the teacher is helping them internalize the science concepts and make them their own. Students need time to explore their own thought processes and questions. It is the teacher's responsibility to pull the students' thoughts together and begin to help students make connections between their thoughts and the concept being explored. These connections are formalized when students are asked to communicate them in writing.

What instructional practices support the development of science notebooks?

Although establishing goals and using the Cycle of Notebook Interaction help establish a focus and a general pattern for notebook use, some students will need additional instruction, supports, or scaffolds to develop their notebooks. Following are strategies that provide general guidance for the notebook. The teacher will need to consider how and when to use these scaffolds and how these change over the course of the year. Looking first at what students are able to do independently allows the teacher to determine how much guidance to provide.

Some strategies to develop notebooks include:

Strategies to develop specific skills within the notebook are provided in Chapter 2.

THINK-ALOUDS: The teacher verbalizes his or her thinking when making a notebook entry. Think-alouds can be done any time during the Cycle of Notebook Interaction to model the thinking process, such as making a prediction or explanation. Think-alouds are also helpful to model the process of recording, why we draw something larger than it is, why we label, or why we organize information in a certain way.

CLASS NOTEBOOK: A class notebook (see Figure 1–4) can be used for several purposes, including modeling how to make a technical drawing, how to lay out physical space on a page, or how to collect class data. Students make entries in the class notebook, serving as models for their peers. These can be kept in a composition book and displayed with a document camera, kept on chart paper, or kept electronically, but students should always have access to them.

PEER MODELING: To develop a repertoire of strategies, students might find it helpful to see models of various methods. Students can explain how they recorded data, answered a focus question, or recorded new questions. Students are less likely to become dependent upon teacher guidance when they are encouraged to share their work with one another rather than learning from teacher-generated models. This allows the teacher to focus first on what students know and what they can learn from each other.

STUDENT-GENERATED CHECKLIST: When students begin to use the notebook, the teacher can guide students in the creation of a checklist for what should be recorded. Although the teacher has predetermined which elements are necessary, having students generate their own list allows them to take greater ownership of their work and serves as a formative assessment opportunity for the teacher.

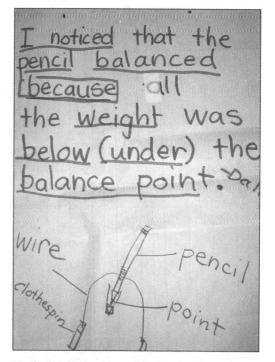

Figure 1–4. An example of a class notebook describing balancing an object

EXAMPLES/NONEXAMPLES: Students need to see quality examples of notebook entries. Provide an example of a quality notebook entry to compare to a nonexample and ask students to discuss what works or is helpful and what needs to be improved in the entry. The idea is for students to determine the characteristics of a good entry. This can be done with any of the elements discussed in Chapter 2.

THINKING POINT: What scaffolds are appropriate for your students?

What instructional practices support English language learners in the development of science notebooks?

For some students, the language of science is further complicated by the fact that English is not their first language. It is helpful to have basic supports available, such as a word wall or vocabulary cards attached to visual pictures depicting the concept or a real object. In addition, further scaffolding can be provided in the form of sentence starters/frames, blackline drawings, and oral rehearsal to support the development of students' understanding of the content and representation of the idea within the science notebooks.

SENTENCE STARTERS/FRAMES: Basic sentence starters or frames can be displayed in the room to provide students with a starting point. Starters such as "I notice . . ." or "I wonder . . ." provide students with a beginning point from which to write in their notebook. These can be expanded upon to include various starters for claims, evidence, and reasoning, or a frame that helps students construct a full explanation. Eventually, frames that help students focus their evidence and reasoning on specific conceptual ideas can replace the generic starters. As with all scaffolds, it is important to change these out over time to promote student independence.

DRAWING STARTER FOR EXPLANATIONS: Although drawings can help convey a student's understanding, they can also be time-consuming and take time away from a written explanation. At times, it might be helpful to provide a blackline master of a system with which students have been working, such as a closed system that contains air, as represented in Figure 1–5. They can use this master to help communicate where air is in the system and then explain in writing what evidence they have to support this idea.

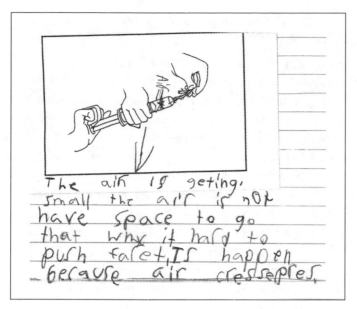

The air is geting,
small the air is not
have space to go
that why it hard to
push facet, Is happen
because air cressepres

Figure 1–5. An example containing a drawing starter followed by a written explanation

ORAL PRACTICE OF OBSERVATIONS/EXPLANATIONS: Some students might be able to explain their thinking in conversation but struggle to convey this in writing due to the time it takes them to physically write. Allow them to capture their idea into an audio-recording device and then listen as they write in their science notebooks. By rehearsing or recording an answer to a focus question first, students can focus on the mechanical aspects of writing it down without forgetting the bigger scientific ideas they are trying to convey.

Creating a Purpose for Notebooks

Why create a purpose?

Notebooks are an important component of scientists' work, and they should be important components of students' investigations. If students do not have a purpose for them, notebooks simply become a busy activity. Students also need a reason to record while they work; otherwise the materials can be too alluring and recording does not take place. Students gain a better appreciation of the notebooks' value if they use them in an authentic manner.

How is an authentic purpose for science notebooks created?

Scientists use their notebooks on a daily basis in the work they do and in conversations with others, similar to the way students use their notebooks. Additionally, scientists make formal presentations on their work to their colleagues. By having students use science notebooks to create a presentation of scientific findings to share with their peers, the teacher establishes an authentic purpose and has a product that can be summatively assessed. These scientific presentations might take the form of oral sharing, an expository text, a report, a slide show presentation, or a poster. Students use their notebooks to reference their questions, procedures, results, explanations, and any new questions they might have while creating their presentations. The following vignette shows how fifth graders shared their understandings of environments. As you read, think about how students used their notebooks as they developed their presentations and how those presentations helped establish a purpose for the notebooks.

My class had been studying different types of environments and how changes would impact plant growth. My content goal was for students to recognize that several environmental factors influence plant growth. Groups of students had planned and begun working on investigations based on questions they generated. A few days into their work, I announced that they would be sharing their investigations and results in the form of a slide show using a familiar computer program. The notebooks served as tools for students to recall their plans, data, thinking, results, and questions as they began to work on their slide shows. Students who recorded a great deal in their notebooks found them very helpful, and those who did not, relied upon others. Following the presentations of their investigations, there was a noticeable change in the documentation of work.

In this vignette, the students were asked to create a formal product based on their work. The data the students needed to access were collected over several days, making the notebook a valuable tool in providing evidence, such as the height of a certain plant at a certain period of time. The teacher provided an experience to help students answer the often asked question, "Why do we have to write all of this down?" on their own.

What is the vision for science notebooks?

Your vision of what notebooks will look like and how they will be used will evolve over time. The following vignette examines one teacher's vision over the first three years of notebook use.

Notebook development for me went from being very structured and teacher-centered to very student-centered over the course of three years. In my first year of implementing notebooks, my goal was student mastery of recording strategies. I wanted to show them all the different recording strategies I knew. I set up the structure for them, told them what to record, and showed them how to record it. Most of the notebooks looked similar, and many students met the goals. Reflecting back, I wonder if students really understood the strategies they used or if they were just following my directions.

The following year, I wanted my students to take more ownership of their notebooks. My goal was for students to select appropriate recording techniques. I introduced them to various recording strategies but left the decisions of what and how to record up to the students. When I looked at their notebooks, I focused on when and how they used the strategies. Over the course of the year, I began to realize that my students were using strategies I introduced to them, but they were not using any other strategies. As students represented their understanding of the content, they used various recording strategies, but the data represented looked similar. At the end of the year, I wondered if the students really understood those strategies or if they used them only because they thought that was the expectation.

In the third year, I gave control of the notebooks over to the students. My goal was for students to use notebooks in a way that made sense to them. At the beginning of the year, students brainstormed ideas for recording strategies, which were posted in the room for reference throughout the year. My mantra for the year became "Record in a way that will make sense to you later." As the year progressed, I provided time for students to share the new strategies they were developing. There were times when I needed to introduce new strategies as well, and I did this through minilessons and modeling. I decided the notebooks belonged to the students, not me, and stopped looking in them to verify everyone was using the same strategies. Instead, I looked at them for their understanding of the science content. The notebooks provided me with evidence of student learning of the scientific content, which I used to inform the decisions I made about instruction.

THINKING POINT: What benefits and limitations are there to various amounts of structure?

Here are two final thinking points for you to consider as you implement science notebooks. These two questions are crucial to understanding your own vision for notebook use in your class.

THINKING POINTS: Where are your students starting? What do you expect to accomplish with science notebooks?

Elements of a
Science Notebook

Although each science notebook entry is unique, there are certain elements that all notebooks contain, such as information about an investigation, the collection and organization of data, questions, explanations, and basic information. Students are encouraged to record these items in a manner that makes sense to them; however, the teacher can also help students develop these elements over time through minilessons or modeling the use of these elements in a class notebook. In addition, the teacher can help students focus these elements on the content by providing students with a focus question that drives the investigation and student recording toward the content rather than the activity. This chapter describes the various ways in which students document their investigations using many scientific practices.

For more on the connections between science notebooks and the disciplinary core ideas of science as well as the practices and crosscutting concepts, see Chapter 5.

Planning Investigations

Students should have opportunities to carry out careful and systematic investigations . . . that develop their ability to observe and measure and to record data. (National Research Council 2012, 60–61)

What does planning an investigation look like?

Science investigations usually involve a plan or abbreviated plan that describes how the inquiry will be conducted. Planning an investigation looks different depending on the grade level at which it takes place as well as students' experiences with planning an investigation. Sometimes the teacher might provide students with a plan to follow. Other times, the class might generate the plan with teacher guidance, and then there are times where small groups of students or individuals create a plan. In the primary grades, the plan will generally be provided or guided by the teacher. In the intermediate grades, it is common to see a greater level of detail and independence in the plan, with students providing very specific directions. The inclusion of plans meets the second goal of science notebooks, to replicate the work of scientists. Just as scientists create plans that detail their work and allow others to replicate it, so too should students include plans with enough detail that somebody else could replicate it in the future. Figure 2–1 demonstrates how one student planned out his investigation.

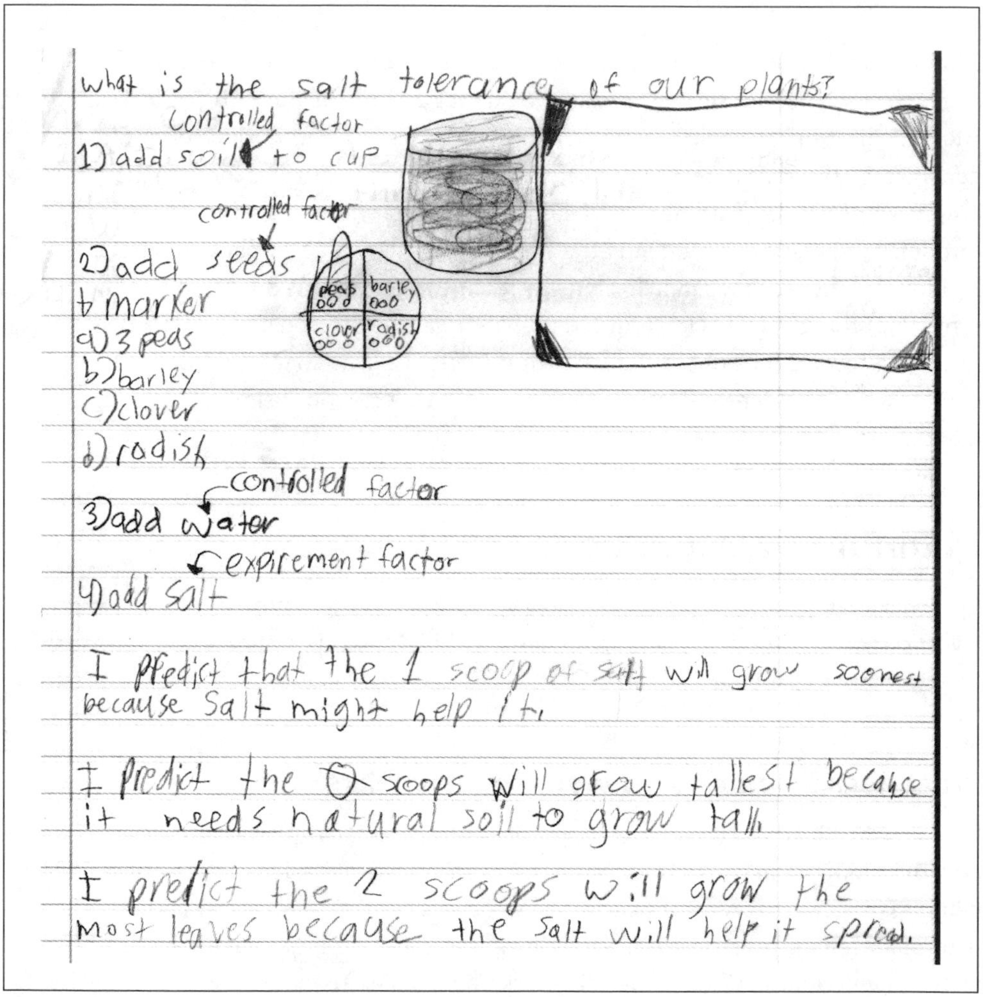

what is the salt tolerance of our plants?
        Controlled factor
1) add soil to cup

        controlled factor
2) add seeds
to marker
a) 3 peas   peas barley
b) barley   clover radish
c) clover
d) radish
        controlled factor
3) add water
        exprement factor
4) add salt

I predict that the 1 scoop of salt will grow soonest because salt might help it.

I predict the 0 scoops will grow tallest because it needs natural soil to grow tall

I predict the 2 scoops will grow the most leaves because the salt will help it spread.

Figure 2–1. Sample of a student's plan for an investigation driven by a focus question provided by the teacher

How can teachers support student planning of investigations?

The teacher might begin the planning process by providing students with a model of the step-by-step procedures students will follow during an investigation. This can be done by thinking aloud the process of planning and recording it in the class notebook or providing students with a sheet that they can glue into their science notebooks that provides step-by-step directions for the investigation. The next level of scaffolding might involve the teacher asking a series of questions to help students construct a plan that includes all of the necessary steps for an investigation. This might be the extent of planning in the primary grades, but at the intermediate grades, students can be asked to work with a partner or small group to create a plan for an investigation. This process can be scaffolded through the use of a planning sheet that outlines the thinking process. The planning sheet might use sequencing words such as "The first thing we are going to do is . . ." or "Once we have . . ." to help students structure their plan in an orderly manner. As students progress in their planning, it is important to decrease the level of scaffolding to promote student independence.

Recording and Organizing Data

What does recording and organizing data look like?

In science, the need arises for students to record and organize the information they are gathering, whether observing the weather or measuring plant growth. In working with these data, there are a wide array of recording and organizational methods available to students. Some of those methods are:

- notes and lists,
- technical drawings and diagrams with labels,
- charts,
- tables,
- graphs, and
- written observations.

The most common methods are probably lists or quick notes that students record in their notebooks to capture the work they are doing. It is important for teachers to remember that these are the students' notes and they should not be subjected to the same criteria put upon other student writing. In real-world note taking, capitalization, punctuation, and grammar are not the focus, the content is; however, notes must be taken in a manner that makes sense. Figures 2–2 and 2–3 demonstrate two different ways students recorded and organized the same data.

THINKING POINT: What expectations will you have for your students as they record? How will your expectations change over time?

Figures 2–2 and **2–3.** Two fifth-grade students represented observations of unknown materials in their own ways.

How do students begin recording and organizing data?

Like scientists, it is important that students become comfortable recording their observations and data while they work in order to reference the information later as they organize and analyze their results. To accomplish this, it is important that notebooks be available during an investigation. This means notebooks might get dirty, wrinkled, and wet; however, this creates the ability to record important information as it is being observed.

When students are first introduced to a material or to science notebooks, they might find it difficult to focus on recording. Therefore, it is important for teachers to provide students with time to experience and explore the material and then encourage recording. The following vignette examines the method one teacher used to introduce notebooks to his second-grade students.

Figures 2–2 and **2–3.** Two fifth-grade students represented observations of unknown materials in their own ways.

Getting my second graders to record data was something that I knew was going to be a pretty hefty time investment; however, it was one that I considered to be worthwhile. It seemed that there were two ways to approach this task: (1) I could focus on the students and allow their ideas to guide the lesson or (2) I could build the lesson around my ideas about how the notebook should be set up and hope the students understood the concept. I decided I would place the focus on the students by watching their actions, listening to their conversations and questions, noticing what they chose to record, and helping them make sense of it.

On the first day of school, my class and I investigated insects, an area typically of interest for the students as well as myself. Before we started looking at the mealworm larva, I introduced the notebooks and set my expectations: students needed to include basic elements, such as a date and title, and any information they felt was important. My goal was to learn what they were capable of doing on their own, so my directions were kept to a minimum. I did not set requirements for recording; their instructions were to record anything they found important. Upon receiving the mealworms, their interest shifted from the notebooks to the mealworms; this I expected. I walked around, listening and discussing with them what they were seeing. They were all actively engaged in observing the mealworms. However, very few recorded their observations. I made a mental note at that time to provide them with time to record.

This vignette demonstrates how it is important for the teacher to know the notebook goal prior to the lesson. To plan for future instruction, the teacher wanted to see what students were capable of observing and recording on their own. The teacher might have been looking for whether the students wrote in a narrative format, expressed their feelings, or used a drawing to represent their observations. The novelty of the mealworms meant that focused recording time was needed at the end to see what students were really capable of on their own.

For many students, notebooks are new and students might struggle with ideas of how and what to record. Students can be excellent resources for one another in this area. One way of exposing students to recording methods is to have students talk with a partner using their notebooks as references. This allows students to see other methods of recording and organizing information in a very informal way. At the end of the lesson, the teacher can invite different students to share their entries with the whole class, providing opportunities for others to see that a variety of techniques can be used effectively. The use of a document camera can enhance this, ensuring that all students are able to see the entry. The following classroom vignette describes this type of sharing and the impact it had upon the class.

After looking at the mealworms, the class met in a circle on the floor to discuss what they observed. A few students brought their notebooks. They started by talking with each other about what they had noticed while observing the mealworms. The few that brought their notebooks shared with a fellow classmate what they had recorded. When we began to share as a group, one of the students who brought his notebook read directly from it. This sharing probably served as a stimulus for many of my students who had not recorded anything. I remember hearing one girl say, "Oh, I should have written that down."

As we finished our first day with the mealworms, I began to think about what might have prevented my students from writing in their notebooks.

- Did they have enough time to write?
- Did they know how to write in this context?
- Did they know what to write?

On the second day, we followed a similar pattern of observation, followed by sharing. As I walked around, I noticed more notebooks being utilized to record observations. I saw one student had included a drawing of the mealworm habitat, so I privately asked if she would share her entry today. I saw another had posed some questions he had about the mealworm, so I asked him to share his entry as well. During the partner discussion, I noticed more students referencing their notebooks as they talked, and I saw that a couple of students had recorded their observations using a list format and others drew pictures. During the whole-group sharing, I asked for volunteers to show how they had recorded and organized their observations. The students I had quietly asked to share did so, as well as a few others. As students shared, I asked them to notice how they had recorded the information. As each student shared, I responded by simply saying, "Thank you for sharing," avoiding any judgments, and I asked the rest of the class if they had any questions, building in opportunities for the students to create dialogue among themselves. At the end of the sharing, we made a list of ways to record information in our notebooks, such as lists and drawings, and types of information to record, such as questions.

Over the next few days, I noticed more and more students recording their observations in their notebooks. The students who had trouble writing recorded with pictures. I began a word bank for commonly used words and placed it in the front of the room for students to refer to when they wrote. By the end of the first week, most students had recorded some information about their mealworms.

In this vignette, the teacher purposefully chose students to share recording strategies to expose students to a variety of strategies. By holding back any judgmental comments, the teacher avoided labeling one strategy as more effective than another. In addition, the word bank provided support for students who might struggle with the new vocabulary. These techniques allowed students to record the information in a manner that was meaningful for them.

THINKING POINT: How do your instructional decisions impact what your students view as important?

When does the teacher actually teach recording strategies?

Getting students to record observations is the initial step; helping them expand upon the depth of their recording is the larger task. To take students beyond the initial stage, it will be important to model a variety of recording and organizational strategies. Students serve as excellent models for one another for methods with which they might have experience; however, additional methods can be provided through teacher modeling. This modeling provides students with resources to draw upon during future investigations. The minilesson, a short ten-minute lesson structured around a recording method that would be appropriate to use with the investigation, is useful here. An organizational tool, such as a table or chart, can be introduced to students by collecting class results and organizing them on the board. For example, while investigating properties of liquids, you or the students recognize the need for an organizational tool. You might choose to introduce a new strategy, such as a chart, to compare the properties of each liquid. After compiling data as a class, you could introduce the chart as one way to organize the data. Next, you could provide a skeleton of a chart, allowing students to determine the heading for each category. Once headings are in place, you might model one or two examples of data entry before providing time for students to complete the chart with guidance.

What about the materials provided in the science curriculum?

Still another way to share recording methods with students is to access resources available in your science curriculum. Some programs provide student sheets to go along with activities; some of these sheets introduce students to new methods for organizing their data. Teachers might utilize these sheets rather than having students reconstruct a chart or table in their notebooks. Students use the sheets to record their data and insert them by folding the sheet in half and stapling it into their science notebooks. Some teachers reduce these sheets on the copier so students can paste them on the pages of their notebooks. Others have used technology to display student sheets to provide those in need of a starting point an idea of one way to organize information without limiting their recording.

Technical Drawings

Technical drawings are "text elements that communicate meaning; they refine, clarify, and extend" (Moline 1995, 16) student entries.

What are technical drawings?

Students are so accustomed to writing, often narrative text, that they do not think of drawing as a way to communicate their understandings. One method of recording that is often overlooked by both teachers and students is the technical drawing. Technical drawings are a powerful way to record observations and share information with others; they include more attention to detail than typical drawings. To draw something well, individuals must observe it closely, noting every small feature and fine line; capturing this type of detail in technical drawings enhances observation skills. The next three vignettes share a second-grade teacher's experience with technical drawings.

> While working with insects, my students had spent some time observing wax worms. However, some of them were experiencing difficulty recording their observations for different reasons; some of them, being English language learners or beginning writers, were limited in the words they had available to them. I realized my students were in need of another tool they could use to record their observations with more detail. We began to explore various drawing techniques.

What is the first step?

Many teachers believe they are not artists and do not feel they can use technical drawings to record their own observations, let alone help their students record observations with technical drawings. When drawing, many people use symbols, such as stick people or the circle flower, to represent an object rather than closely observing that object and drawing exactly what they see. Figures 2–4 and 2–5 show the difference between a symbol and a technical

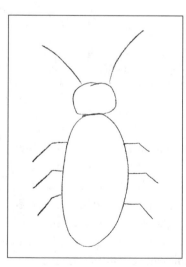

Figure 2–4. Symbol of an insect

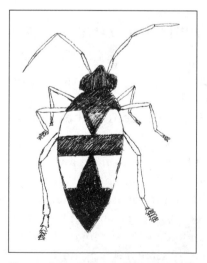

Figure 2–5. Technical drawing of a milkweed bug

drawing. However, with a little practice and guidance, everyone can experience success with technical drawings and go beyond recording a symbol to recording a detailed drawing.

To help students be successful with technical drawings, teachers need to offer them support. A guided drawing is a process in which the teacher and students look at an object together and discuss what they see. The teacher draws the object on the board or in the class notebook and encourages students to draw along on their own papers. At this beginning point, many of the drawings will look similar; this is fine. Through guided drawings, students gain experience with the tools of drawing as well as realize the observational skills needed to draw an object accurately. This initial support is crucial. If teachers simply ask students to draw technically without providing them with the tools, the outcome will be frustration for both the teacher and the students.

To begin guided drawings, the teacher and the students look closely at the object that is to be drawn. They notice how parts of the object (a head, a wing, etc.) resemble basic shapes (square, rectangle, circle, oval, triangle, rhombus). They examine the entire object, noting the various shapes that are present, and choose the largest or main shape of the object and draw that on the paper. Once it is down on the paper, the teacher and students soften the sides or reconfigure it slightly so the appearance matches that of the object more closely. They then continue to add to their drawings by using basic shapes that are modified slightly to more closely match the object. This process, or the stages of a technical drawing, is shown in Figure 2–6.

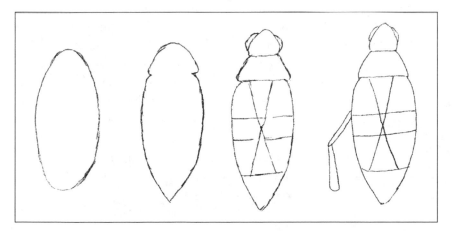

Figure 2–6. Beginning stages for technical drawing of a milkweed bug

What other types of support do students need?

A support that many find helpful to use is a blackline master of the object being drawn. It is easier to see lines that have already been drawn than it is to find lines on an object. Many curricula offer drawings of the various materials with which students are working. Using a copier, the teacher enlarges these drawings, if needed, to a point that students can easily see the shapes and lines present. When using a blackline master to guide the drawing, it is important for the teacher to emphasize that this is one interpretation of the way the object looks and that it is only a guide. The students must examine the original object closely, perhaps with the use of a hand lens, and add details that might be different from those included on the blackline copy.

> Through close examination of a blackline master, my students began to look at the wax worm differently. Looking for shapes allowed them to describe it more accurately than their previous description of "round." When comparing the actual wax worm with the blackline representation, the students started to see that different parts of the wax worm were different shades and the different parts had features they had not noticed. Using hand lenses, they saw hair extending from the wax worm's body. They noticed "holes" on the sides of the wax worms. These features were then incorporated into their drawings.

Figure 2–7 shows one student's drawing from this lesson.

Proportion is another important factor to examine. To draw an object accurately, students need to pay attention to the proportions of the object. When drawing an insect, students look closely at the size of the head in comparison with the body. Then they examine where the legs are attached to the body. Teachers can ask questions to focus students and help them to record their observations more accurately. For example: "Are there markings on the body that would help in placing the legs? How far apart are the legs? Where does one leg begin and end in relationship to another?"

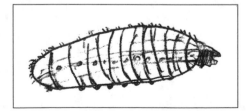

Figure 2–7. A second grader's technical drawing of a wax worm

THINKING POINT: What opportunities within your curriculum allow students to use technical drawings?

Once students understand the techniques of technical drawings, it is important that the teacher builds in opportunities for practice. Many students find it easy to communicate with drawings, but those who might still not consider themselves artists might forgo technical drawings unless encouraged to include them in their notebooks. Later, when students are comfortable with drawing, they will begin to freely include technical drawings in their notebook entries. They will use the tools mentioned earlier (proportion, shapes, blackline masters) to create original drawings. Be patient and understand that completing technical drawings is worth the time they take. It is important that students be provided with the time to record their observations by drawing and that they are sometimes asked to represent their thinking using drawings.

> Although some students (as well as myself) could not draw very well, I noticed that looking at the details and attempting to re-create them on paper brought forth new ideas and structures, such as spiracles. Throughout the year, my students had many opportunities to draw many different things. Often they asked if they could draw the details like they did with the wax worms. They did not always include such details, but when they had the time, they did. They noticed more and more details and recorded more and more details, not just with words, but also with drawings.

Not only does technical drawing support those at the emerging stage of language development, but it helps all students notice and include details. By scaffolding the instruction and providing the students with techniques for drawing, the teacher acknowledges drawings as a means of visual literacy.

THINKING POINT: How do technical drawings fit in with how you teach science?

What other ways are technical drawings used to enhance understanding?

Technical drawings provide a wealth of information to the readers. Drawings can be enhanced through the use of labels. "Labeled diagrams work like glossaries and they can be a more powerful tool than vocabulary lists . . . the words are supported by the pictures which help to define or explain the meanings of the words especially for very young students or those students who are learning English as a second language" (Moline 1995, 23). By asking students to draw and label an object rather than label a worksheet, teachers gain a better idea of the students' understanding and of what they are able to do independently. The components students include in their drawings, or those components they leave out, provide the teacher with a window into what children see as important. Creating their own drawings with labels is far more challenging and worthwhile than labeling existing diagrams and allows students to utilize informal terms or formal vocabulary.

Students' Questions

When we interact with the materials, there are inherent questions in our actions with those materials. (Rebecca Dyasi, personal communication, June 13, 2002)

What are students' questions?

In science, students raise different types of questions; some questions are about directions or procedures, and others capture a curiosity—a need to know why something is the way it is. Questioning takes place between students as well as between the students and the teacher. There are also times when the questions students ask are never spoken nor documented in writing. Obviously, some students' questions lend themselves to science investigation more than others. As teachers of science, it is important to capitalize on this curiosity and students' natural questions, bringing awareness to questions that can be investigated and working with students to recognize and record them.

What can be done to help students recognize their questions?

Often, students don't recognize that they have a question they are exploring; rather, they see it simply as an attempt to determine how something works. When students are manipulating materials, the teacher can help students recognize the questions they are asking. By talking with them, the teacher can discover what their students are thinking and help them reword their thoughts as questions. The following vignette describes how a fifth-grade teacher guided a group of students to recognize their questions.

> As my students were exploring pendulums, I noticed a group that was changing the height from which the pendulum was dropped. I went over to their table and asked them what they were investigating. The students responded, "We want to see if it will swing longer if we drop it from up here" (indicating a higher location than the original starting point).
>   "Oh, so you want to see how changing the starting position affects the length of time the pendulum swings?" By rephrasing the question in this way, I changed it from a yes-or-no question to an open-ended question.

How do I help students record questions that are worthy of investigation?

Once students begin to ask their own questions, the teacher should model the importance of capturing these questions for future reference. A class "research board" serves as a place to capture students' questions. During the early stages of forming questions, students often create queries that can be answered with yes or no. It is important to call their attention to this and begin to work at rephrasing these questions to make them more open-ended because open-ended questions allow thinking to be extended beyond the initial question. If a child asks, "Do turtles like lettuce?" the teacher might rephrase it as "What food does the turtle prefer?"

As students become comfortable asking open-ended questions, they then begin to explore the difference between questions for investigation and questions that require other types of research. One way to do this is to have the students record their questions on sentence strips. The teacher then categorizes the questions with the class according to those that can be answered by further work with the materials versus those that require consulting an expert (book, person, Internet, etc.). Once students have an idea of the two categories, they can continue to sort their questions. It is important for students to understand the difference between the two types of questions to continue to investigate independently. As you read the following vignette, note how the teacher helped her students sort and refine their questions.

> After providing students with opportunities to develop questions, I asked them to share their questions with one or two of their peers. This sharing time allowed students to hear what others were exploring while exposing them to various questioning styles. As other students' questions sparked their interest, students began recording them in their own notebooks. I then asked students to select two or three questions from their notebooks to record on sentence strips, which they hung around the room. Together they sorted the questions into the teacher-selected categories of "can be answered by working with the materials," "must be answered by an expert or book," and "not sure." The students and I reworded those questions that were placed in the "not sure" category and then added them to one of the two other columns. At this point, students had created questions they could investigate.

In this vignette, the teacher helped students come up with questions they could investigate themselves. Asking open-ended questions is difficult to do, even for many adults, so it is important to help students develop these types of questions. Having such questions within their notebooks allows students to refer back to them throughout their investigation, serves as a source from which they can develop new investigations, and provides teachers with a record of students' curiosities.

THINKING POINT: What are reasonable expectations for your students in terms of developing and recording questions that can be investigated?

What do students do with their questions once they are recorded?

Questions are the heart of a scientific investigation. The investigation might actually begin with a teacher- or program-generated question, but it is the students' questions that fuel their desire to know more and do more with their investigations. Students might come to the end of an investigation to find that they are only just beginning and that the work they have done has actually generated more questions than it answered. By keeping those questions in their notebooks, students are able to refer back to them during future investigations, as scientists do, and hopefully investigate and answer their own questions. Figure 2–8 shows how one student recorded questions within the notebook.

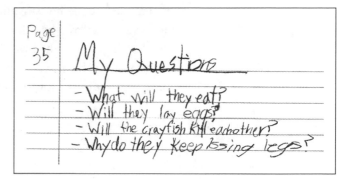

Figure 2–8. A sample of recorded questions in a third grader's notebook

Recording Thinking

What does it mean to record thinking?

As students work in science, they are gathering data that are essential to their work. At some point, it is important that they attempt to make sense of their data, examine what the data mean and why their results might differ from others, and decide how they plan to proceed. By asking students to record their thinking, teachers are asking them to do much more than simply reflect on the activity—they are asking their students to reflect on their thought processes and how they came to their way of thinking, to use data collected as evidence to support or change ideas about concepts, and to share questions they now have.

What does it look like when students record their thinking?

Although some students might record their thoughts using complete sentences, others will use fragments. Students' thinking might be recorded as predictions, conjectures, hypotheses, explanations, or drawings. Some students embed their thinking throughout their work and others synthesize their thoughts at the end. It is important to remember that children are individuals and need to record their thinking in a way that makes sense to them, as shown in Figures 2–9 and 2–10.

Thinking takes place before, during, and after an investigation. Thinking before the investigation involves planning the investigation, predicting what might happen, and connecting ideas to prior experiences. Considering outcomes before the investigation guides students to look for evidence that will prove or disprove their thinking during their work. How students record their thinking during the investigation differs from how they record observations; students have to not only communicate what they are observing but interpret that information and process it. Initially, this might be difficult for

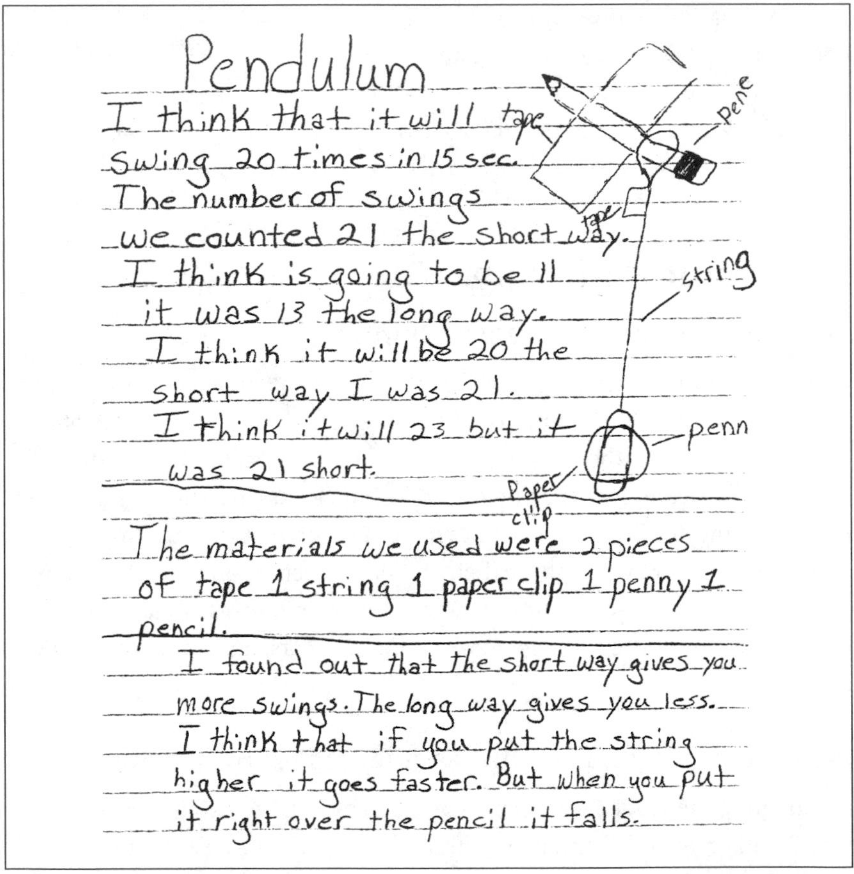

Pendulum

I think that it will swing 20 times in 15 sec.
The number of swings we counted 21 the short way.
I think is going to be 11 it was 13 the long way.
I think it will be 20 the short way I was 21.
I think it will 23 but it was 21 short.

The materials we used were 2 pieces of tape 1 string 1 paper clip 1 penny 1 pencil.

I found out that the short way gives you more swings. The long way gives you less.
I think that if you put the string higher it goes faster. But when you put it right over the pencil it falls.

Figure 2–9. A record of a fifth grader's thinking while working with pendulums for the first time the students; however, with time and practice they will improve. After the investigation, students record their thinking as

- ◉ reflections on what they noticed and how that might impact future investigations;
- ◉ concrete thoughts based on the evidence gathered;
- ◉ new understandings based on what they have learned;
- ◉ explanations that contain a claim, evidence, and reasoning;
- ◉ questions resulting from the recognition of gaps in their thinking; or
- ◉ ideas of what they will try next.

Figure 2–10. A first grader's record of thinking while working with the concept of balance and stability

How much time is needed for students to record their thinking?

Recording thinking is not an easy task for students; many understand what is happening but struggle when it comes to translating their thoughts into words. One way to support students is to provide them with time to discuss and write with a partner or small group about their ideas. Students should be encouraged and given time to write in their notebooks before, during, and after an investigation. They cannot be expected to synthesize their thinking in thirty seconds; time must be built into the lesson. How this is incorporated into the lesson varies. Sometimes specific time needs to be set aside for students to record their thinking, such as when working with highly intriguing materials or investigations that occur quickly, and at other times it needs to be embedded in the investigation. If students do not have time to record their thinking, their notebooks might become just logs of data.

What does it look like when students record explanations?

Scientists provide explanations for the way the world behaves based on their work. In replicating the work of scientists, it is important that students participate in this important practice and provide explanations based on their work for the way the world behaves. At the elementary level, scientific explanations contain a claim, evidence, and reasoning (Zembal-Saul, McNeill, and Hershberger 2013). The claim is a statement that provides an answer to the investigation focus question. Evidence can take the shape of quantitative or qualitative data the students have gathered throughout the investigation. For the data to be considered evidence, they should support the claim and be relevant. Finally, reasoning links the claim and evidence, serving as a means of justification of why the student has come to that claim or answer, ideally linking the idea to the bigger scientific concept. Younger students might focus more on the claims and evidence within their science notebooks, as reasoning is a more complex process. Figures 2–11 and 2–12 show two students' explanations, followed by a breakdown of their claim, evidence, and reasoning.

In Figure 2–11, the student made the claim that the best design for a solar water heater was black, based on evidence from his graph that "black covered went up the highest," and he supported this idea with his reasoning that "black absorbed more light." In Figure 2–12, the student's claim "that air slows down the parachute" was supported by the evidence that "when I dropped the parachute it fell down slowly" and the reasoning that "this happens because air resistance slows the parachute."

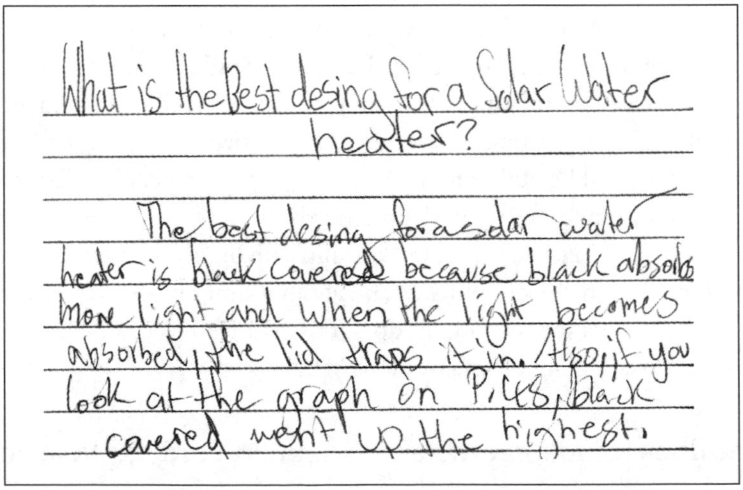
What is the Best desing for a Solar Water heater?

The best desing forasolar water heater is black covered because black absorbs more light and when the light becomes absorbed, the lid traps it in. Also, if you look at the graph on P.48, black covered went up the highest.

Figure 2–11. A fifth-grade student's explanation on the best material to use for a solar water heater

How can the teacher support student development of explanations?

The language of science, including that used to formulate explanations, is often new to students. Even those who are native speakers might struggle to develop sound scientific explanations. Several protocols exist (Fulwiler 2007, 2011; Norton-Meier et al. 2008; Zembal-Saul, McNeill, and Hershberger 2013) to help students develop the language associated with the scientific practice of developing scientific explanations. An important aspect of an explanation is the question students are attempting to answer; therefore, think carefully about the focus question that guides the investigation, as it will also guide the development of the explanation. You can scaffold explanations by providing sentence starters or frames. Generic starters can be useful, but more specific frames might help the students focus on the bigger scientific ideas. As with all scaffolds, it is important to change them over time, removing the scaffolding gradually, to develop student independence. In addition, teachers can further support the development of explanations by modeling the process. In the following vignette, consider how the fourth-grade teacher supported students in the development of an explanation.

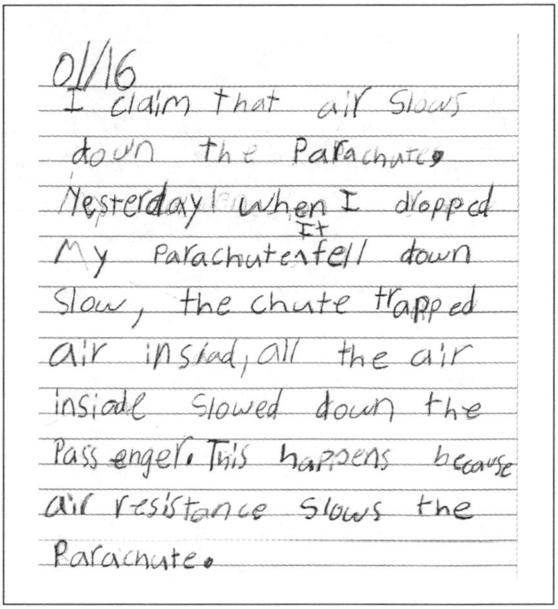

Figure 2–12. A second grader's explanation about why a parachute descends slowly

In preparation for our schoolwide science conference, I decided to model the scientific practices of collecting, analyzing, and interpreting data with my students. To do this, I engaged them in a guided inquiry on ultraviolet (UV) beads. UV beads change color in response to UV light. After some exploration with the beads, we developed a question, "What lightbulbs affect the color of the UV beads similar to the way the Sun affects their color?" We also developed a plan, and the students investigated the effect of various

Bead Data

Trial	Black Light	GrowLab Light
1	All beads changed - bright like the sun	Some bead changed color
2	All beads changed - a little color	No beads changed
3	Only the blue bead changed	Only one bead changed color

Scale of Bead Brightness

1	2	3	4
No Change	1-2 beads changed little color	all beads changed medium color	all beads changed bright, like in the sun

Trial	Blacklight	GrowLab	Flashlight	Regular Light	Sun
1	3	2	1	2	4
2	3	3	1	2	4
3	3	2	1	2	4

Figure 2–13. Example of a class notebook entry containing data from an investigation on UV beads

light sources on the UV beads within their small groups. They had recorded their data, and I recognized that the data were not displayed in a way that would allow for analysis. Based on this, I made the decision to model the organization of the data in the class notebook. To analyze the data, I asked a series of questions that guided the students to determine under what condition the beads did or did not look similar to the beads in the Sun (see Figure 2–13).

Once we had our data analyzed, we were ready to construct an explanation. I called the students to the floor and started by reviewing the class data. To help students understand the components of an explanation, I had created and hung a chart in the classroom that identified claims, evidence, and reasoning. I shared that we needed to make a claim, which was an answer to our question. The students provided various suggestions, and we finally settled on a group claim, which I entered into the class notebook (see Figure 2–14). I drew a box around this text, so the students could associate it with the definition of a claim on our class chart. Next, we looked at our data and determined what evidence we had to support our claim. Again, students helped craft one statement for our evidence. I drew a single line under this text to match the definition of evidence on our chart. Finally,

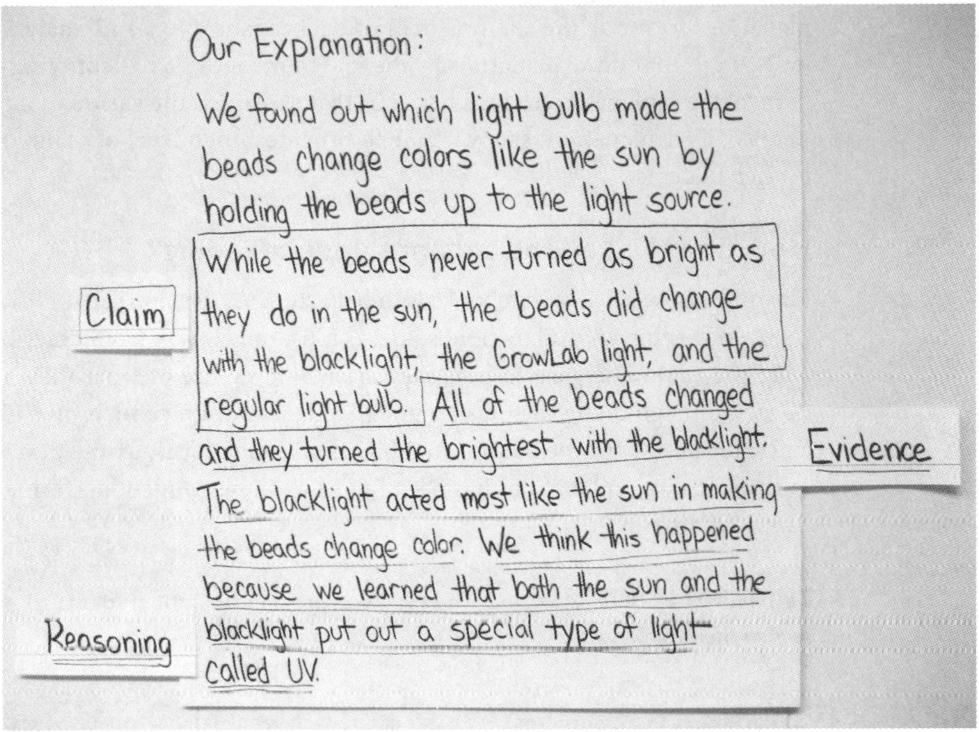

Our Explanation:

We found out which light bulb made the beads change colors like the sun by holding the beads up to the light source.

Claim
While the beads never turned as bright as they do in the sun, the beads did change with the blacklight, the GrowLab light, and the regular light bulb.

Evidence
All of the beads changed and they turned the brightest with the blacklight. The blacklight acted most like the sun in making the beads change color.

Reasoning
We think this happened because we learned that both the sun and the blacklight put out a special type of light called UV.

Figure 2–14. Example of a class notebook entry containing an explanation for an investigation on UV beads

the students provided their reasoning or justification as to why they thought this light source affected the color in a manner similar to the sun. I wrote this up and drew two lines under the text to match the definition of reasoning on our chart. I sent the students back to their seat to write their own explanations based on the data they had in their science notebooks, emphasizing that although the class explanation might help them with how to write their own explanation, it did not represent their data and they needed to write their own explanations rather than copying the class one into their notebooks.

Color can be used as an alternative way to identify the claim, evidence, and reasoning.

In this vignette, the teacher supported her students in constructing explanations by modeling the practices of data organization and analysis as well as creating an explanation in the class notebook. By identifying the parts of the explanation to match a chart that explained the various components of an explanation, she was able to provide a high level of scaffolding for her students.

How do explanations enhance understanding?

The first goal of science notebooks is to help students develop scientific concepts. In creating an explanation, students must move away from describing what they did in science to how they are making sense of what they have learned through doing the investigation. Students must take their own ideas and attempt to connect them to the bigger scientific ideas, as the development of quality explanations has been linked to higher student performance (Ruiz-Primo et al. 2010).

THINKING POINT: How and when will you provide time for students to record their thinking?

Other Elements

What else might be included in science notebooks?

Science notebooks are collections of information gathered over time. There are some basic elements of notebooks that help document the process students are going through and should be included with every entry. These include (1) date, (2) time, and (3) heading (topic, title, or question). Each of these elements aids students when they look back at entries and analyze their data; therefore, it is a good idea to establish the habit of including these elements with every entry.

Other elements are not essential to science notebooks; however, they might be powerful tools for the students to use from time to time. When working with materials students might find it helpful to collect samples, when appropriate, and include them in their entries. A leaf sample, insect molt, or results from a chromatography experiment might be taped in for future reference. When a sample is not a viable option, students might want to consider including a rubbing of the object to capture the texture of it.

There are times when neither a sample nor a rubbing is possible and a drawing would be too difficult. In these situations, a photo might capture the event. Students like to include photos in their notebooks, so it is important for teachers to think carefully about the use of this technology. For some items drawings might be more appropriate than photos, as drawings require close observation and attention to detail.

Photos can also be used to capture those moments when students are so engaged with the materials that recording in their notebooks would be difficult. The photos can be inserted into their science notebooks, and students can use them as prompts to write about the experience. This type of writing is called *photojournalism* and is a motivating tool for students. Figure 2–15 shows a sample of photojournalism.

The thing I was testing is that I was pouring water down a slope. I thought the water would go down the slope and the way the ground is slanted for example if it were slanted to the left the water would go to the left.

Figure 2–15. Sample of photojournalism

Newer technologies can also be used to support notebook entries. Students might be encouraged to take their own photos or video during an investigation to make a point. They might record their response to a focus question and listen to it to determine if their response accurately conveys their understanding prior to putting the recording in their science notebook. These technologies might also help students organize their data into tables and graphs. The opportunities to support notebook entries with technology will change as rapidly as the technology advances. Encourage students to use technology in a way that will further their thinking and enhance their entries in a meaningful manner.

THINKING POINT: When is a photograph or technology a hindrance and when is it a help in learning the science content?

It is important that students are able to recall the materials they worked with in an experiment; however, students do not always need to write a materials list. Quite often students include the materials they used within the explanation of what they did or within drawings and the reader needs only to extract that information, as shown in Figure 2–16.

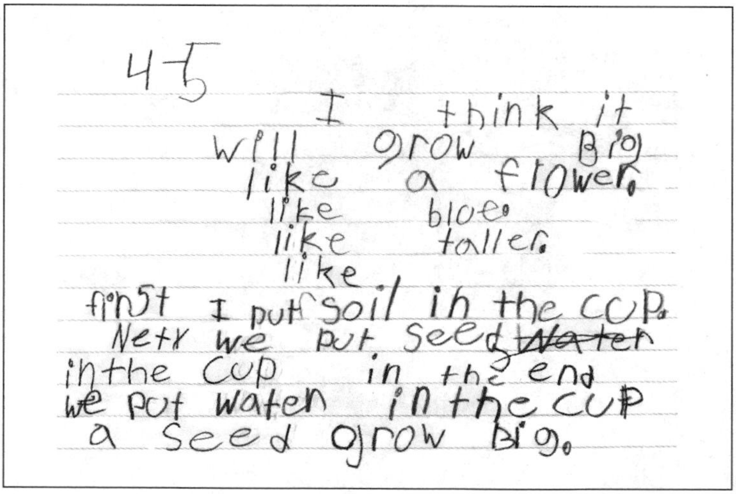
4-5
I think it
will grow Big
like a flower.
like bloe.
like taller.
like
first I put soil in the cup.
Netr we put seed ~~water~~
in the cup in the end
we put waten in the cup
a seed grow Big.

Figure 2–16. A first-grade student embeds the materials used while writing about the investigation.

Elementary teachers are always looking for ways to integrate curricula and many teachers have pulled various features of expository text into science notebooks. These include the table of contents, glossary, and index. If teachers choose to incorporate these features, they need to consider how they will be used and if the time spent setting them up will be worthwhile.

Chapter 6, "Literacy Connections," offers information on using science notebooks as a context for literacy development.

THINKING POINT: How will students make use of expository text features (glossary, index, etc.) in future lessons?

There are several elements to a science notebook. Throughout the Cycle of Notebook Interaction, the teacher incorporates these elements and supports their use in the documentation of the work and communication of their understanding. As students become more familiar with these notebook elements, their skills and content understanding will grow. In the next chapter, we offer some suggestions for how to assess and monitor that progress.

3

Signs of Student Progress

Science notebooks are meant to be tools for students, used during science investigations and discussions as records of information and resources in conversations. With support and scaffolding, the science notebook becomes a powerful learning tool for students as they plan investigations, collect data and questions, analyze their data, and construct explanations and arguments. As students use their science notebooks, they become more adept with scientific and engineering practices, and progress can be seen in both their documentation skills and their understanding of the content.

This progress can be monitored through a formative assessment process, where the teacher examines notebook entries on a regular basis to determine where students are in their understandings and what they are able to do, and then uses this information to determine future instruction. Such assessment may take place "on-the-fly" (Shavelson et al. 2008, 23), as teachers read notebook entries, listen to student conversations, or talk one-on-one with a student, or be planned, such as asking students to write a response to a focus question. Whatever form it takes, formative assessment of the notebooks is essential to help students use them in the most effective manner and to monitor student understanding of the content. In addition, teachers can have students routinely assess their work and set goals for themselves as learners. To help clarify what teachers should look for in terms of notebook development and conceptual understanding, this chapter examines how students progress with notebooks from beginning to more advanced stages of use.

> We define the formative assessment process as one in which the teacher determines goals, implements the lesson, reviews student work, gains insight into student understanding, uses that information to inform instruction, provides students with feedback, and allows time for revision.

Looking at Science Notebooks

How can the science notebook inform instruction?

To inform instruction, notebooks must be examined on a regular basis. By allowing students some time to make sense of the notebook on their own, teachers are able to see what students can do independently. When support or scaffolds are provided, it is important to remember that the outcome is a result of the structure afforded and does not offer insight into what the students are able to do independently. Although students might need assistance in developing the science notebook, it is also important to provide them with opportunities to demonstrate what they can do independently.

When collecting notebooks, it can be helpful to ask students to leave their notebook open to, or to tag, the specific page to be examined, as this makes the process easier. In addition, if collecting a class set of notebooks is cumbersome, you might ask students to leave them open on their desks or collect a smaller set of notebooks each night. These sets can be determined by colored dots on the front of the notebook or by classroom groupings. For teachers who teach multiple science classes, students can write particular responses on index cards, allowing for the collection of the cards rather than multiple class sets of notebooks. These cards can then be taped into the notebook later.

When looking at science notebooks, it is important to have a goal. That goal might focus on the students' notebook skills, such as their ability to record in chronological order or organize a set of collected data, or on their conceptual understandings of the scientific content being taught. Both play important roles. Teachers can use this goal to determine what students know and are able to do and provide feedback to students about their progress by placing self-stick notes on pages with questions that encourage students to think about their entries. If it is clear that several students in the class do not understand a concept or skill, then future instruction can be adjusted to accommodate those students or to provide a different experience for the entire class. If an important element of the notebook is missing, the teacher could do a minilesson on that specific element and model it within the class notebook. Such feedback should help the students move forward with their skill development and/or their understanding of the scientific content. Teachers might need to help students make sense of the feedback and allot time for students to revise their work by providing opportunities such as talking about the concept with other students and adding information to their notebooks. Students could also use this information to set goals for themselves for their notebook use. Most importantly, the teacher needs to select a specific action based on the student work to improve conceptual understanding, communication skills, or documentation of work in the notebook.

This process of examining the notebooks and providing feedback is meant to be formative in nature and grades should not be assigned during this process. The notebook is a personal tool for the student and should be

Some general strategies are described here. More specific strategies for improving communication and documentation skills are shared in Chapters 1 and 2.

meaningful to that student. When students begin focusing on grades, some of this meaning can be lost, turning the notebook into a bound workbook rather than a personal learning tool.

THINKING POINT: How and when will you collect science notebooks for formative assessment purposes?

Progress in Developing Notebook Documentation Skills

What evidence of progress is there in students' notebook documentation skills?

Science notebooks take time to develop and will not look perfect in the beginning. Students might struggle with recording information or referring back to their notebook for information. You can help students develop these skills by incorporating the Cycle of Notebook Interaction, described in Chapter 1, as well as providing various supports and scaffolds, such as thinking aloud while making a class notebook entry or providing organizing templates in which to put data. As the teacher changes the scaffolds over time, students develop independence and progress in their skills related to documentation. (For more on supports and scaffolds see Chapter 2.)

PREDICTING

Prediction is the use of knowledge to identify and explain observations, or changes, in advance. (National Research Council 1996, 116)

Too often, students equate making a prediction with guessing; they attempt to decide an outcome without the benefit of any experiences on which to base the decision. For this reason, students' predictions might begin as nothing more than random guessing. Their predictions might make little sense in the scheme of their notebooks. Without the fundamental understanding of predictions, students sometimes become frustrated when confronted with data that do not match their prediction. At this beginning stage, students often want their predictions to be correct, so they might look for indications of this and end up reading more into the data or manipulating those data to make them match their ideas. Other students might actually alter their predictions, as evidenced by erasing or crossing out, after observing an event to ensure that they are correct. At this point, students struggle with the purpose of predictions and with recording them in their notebooks.

As students gain an understanding of what it means to predict, they progress by using their prior experiences when making predictions. Students refer to previous notebook entries and provide evidence to support their thinking. Predictions begin to make sense in their entries and are not entered haphazardly. There is no longer a sense that predictions must be changed to be correct; rather, students revisit their predictions as they gather data and express new ideas based on evidence. They no longer equate information that does not agree with their prediction with being wrong, but rather look at it as a learning opportunity.

At this point, students might still need prompting to make a prediction, as it is not yet automatic. As students progress further, they recognize the value in recording their predictions, and predictions become a natural part of their scientific entries, as Figure 3–1 demonstrates. Although not always

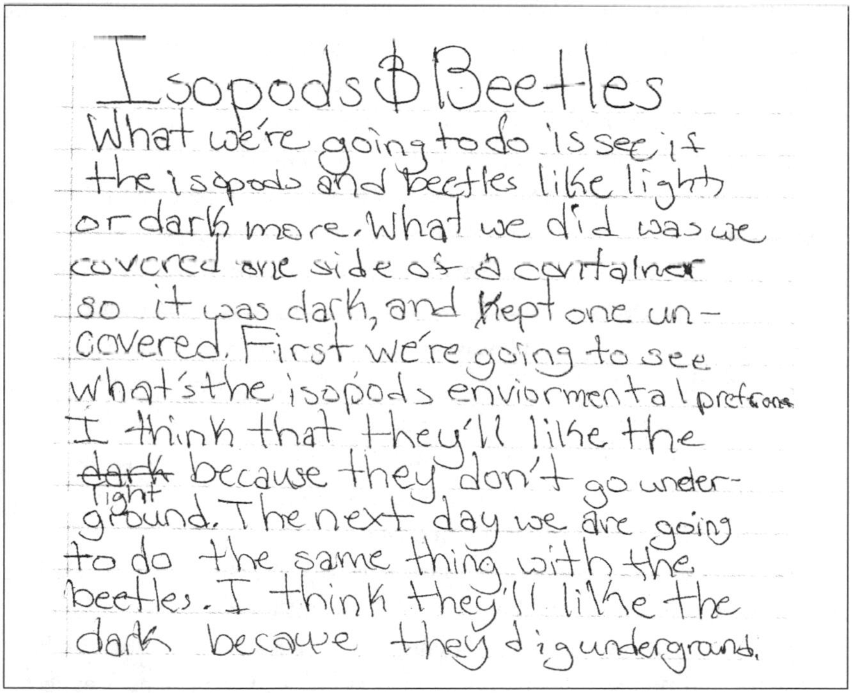
Isopods & Beetles
What we're going to do is see if the isopods and beetles like light or dark more. What we did was we covered one side of a container so it was dark, and kept one un-covered. First we're going to see what's the isopods enviormental prefrens I think that they'll like the ~~dark~~ light because they don't go under-ground. The next day we are going to do the same thing with the beetles. I think they'll like the dark becawe they dig undergrand.

Figure 3–1. A fifth-grade student considers what the outcome of the investigation will be.

accurate, their predictions are supported by evidence from previous experiences with the materials. They realize their predictions should be examined and they should base future predictions on the knowledge learned from previous experiences.

RECORDING AND ORGANIZING DATA

At the elementary level, students need support to recognize the need to record observations—whether in drawings, words, or numbers—and to share them with others. As they engage in scientific inquiry more deeply, they should begin to collect categorical or numerical data for presentation in forms that facilitate interpretation, such as tables and graphs. (National Research Council 2012, 63)

When students begin using notebooks, they might not focus on the data as a whole but instead focus on individual pieces. Students are often busy exploring the materials and might not think to record their ideas unless prompted to do so by the teacher. Data collection might not be focused and data are often entered randomly rather than in an organized manner. This makes it difficult to revisit information and make sense of it later. Materials and procedures and other elements are often forgotten and instead students focus on the results, which might be a blend of data and fictional thoughts.

After some time, students begin to show progress by experimenting with different methods of data collection; however, some might still rely on the teacher's directions for guidance with their entries. In addition to recording their ideas in lists, students might draw pictures with labels or descriptions, develop simple data tables, write sentences to describe their thinking, or create graphic organizers. They begin to organize their information, using titles for their entries and grouping sections together. This organization allows them to utilize the data later and build upon their understandings. Data collection is not the sole focus, and students might now begin to reference procedures and/or materials in their entries.

As students become more comfortable with notebooks, their method of recording progresses by taking several different forms, such as drawings, sentences, charts, and tables. As students feel more confident in their abilities to observe and record information, they often exceed the teacher's expectations. There is the realization that organization helps make sense of data, so students strive to organize their entries in a meaningful manner. They consider the recording method prior to recording the information, and they can justify the appropriateness of one method over another. Students strive to include information in their entries so they or someone else might be able to replicate their work in the future.

THINKING POINT: Looking at Figures 3–2 and 3–3, what can you tell about this student's progression over the course of the year?

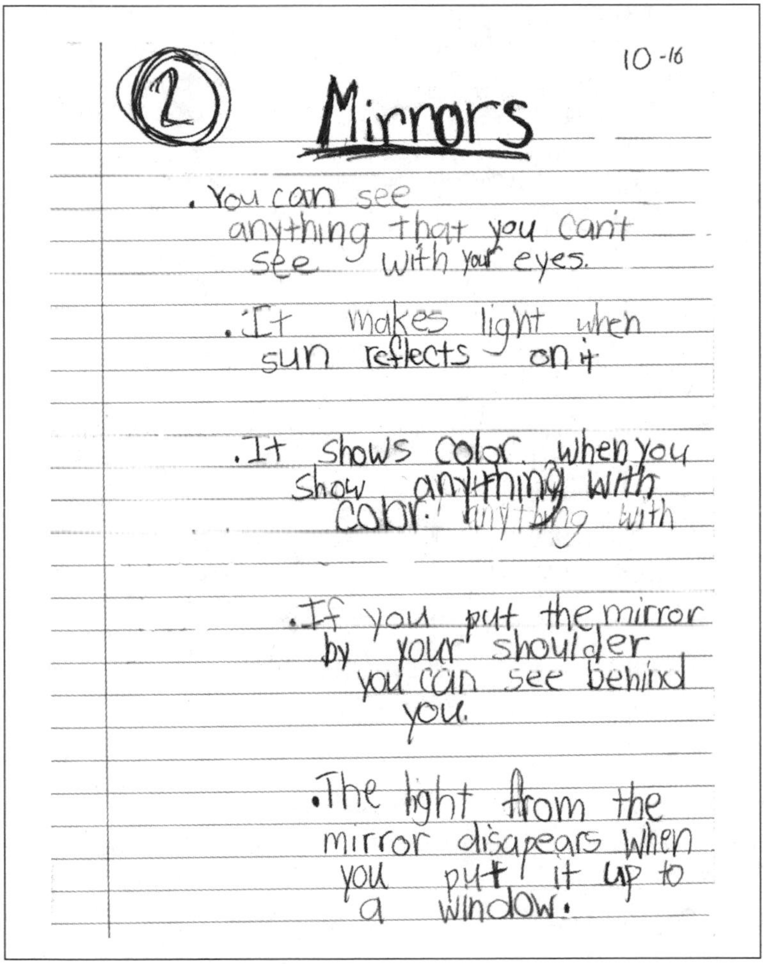
2
10-16
Mirrors
. You can see anything that you can't see with your eyes.
. It makes light when sun reflects on it
. It shows color when you show anything with color.
. If you put the mirror by your shoulder you can see behind you.
. The light from the mirror disapears when you put it up to a window.

Figure 3–2. A third grader's notebook in October

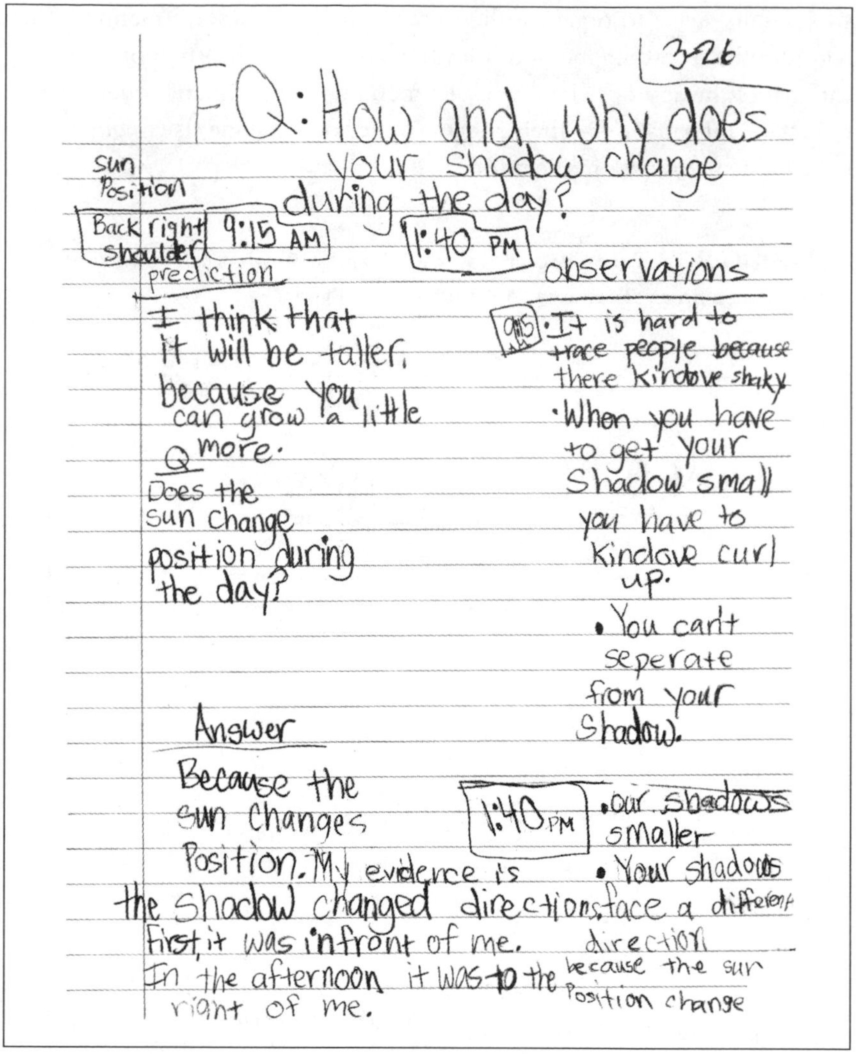

Figure 3–3. The same student's notebook in March

DRAWING

[I]nitial sketches and single-word descriptions lead to increasingly more detailed drawings and richer verbal descriptions. (National Research Council 1996, 123)

Students' drawings usually begin as symbols of objects, such as daisy-type flowers or stick figures. The symbols represent the materials but do not include details specific to the object being drawn. Students are usually familiar with drawing for enjoyment but often do not understand the significance of drawing for understanding. Therefore, materials might be drawn in imaginary scenes or color used inaccurately, such as coloring a mealworm purple or orange. Students might label their drawings, but they are not sure of the purpose of labels at this point and end up labeling everything on their drawings rather than specific aspects.

Students show progress as they begin to see drawings as learning tools. They pay attention to details, such as drawing leaf veins or recording segments in an insect's leg. They pay attention to color and proportion for a more accurate representation of the material. They now use labels sparingly to clarify important aspects of their drawings. There is the realization that drawing portions of the material in greater detail provides more information than drawing the entire object.

With experience, students begin using drawing techniques such as shapes and proportion to provide detail in their work. They see labels as tools to enhance the drawings and define terminology. Beyond labels, students might begin to use captions to expand upon the entry, for example, "Bird's-eye view of isopod habitat." Students begin to manipulate the objects and draw them from various perspectives or in different scales. They use color and shading techniques to better depict the characteristics of the object. Students might additionally represent their conceptual models through drawings showing not just what can be seen, but their thinking about what is unseen.

In the following vignette, a teacher describes how first-grade students progressed as they worked with drawings in their notebook entries. What do the students' drawings show about their changing understanding and skill in using notebooks?

> Knowing that my students had had limited exposure to various drawing techniques, I was curious to see how they would record their observations as we examined plant structures. I noticed some of the drawings contained color but seemed to lack details. The plants being observed had leaves with many shades of green; however, in their notebooks many of the students colored the leaves a solid green and seemed to miss the intricate patterns created by the variation in color. The drawings also seemed to consist

of the basic outlines of the plants and contained few other internal details.

I decided to end the students' observations a little early, so that we could make a class notebook entry of what we had observed so far. As students shared their observations and I recorded in the notebook, I did a think-aloud of how I noticed the leaves had veins that made them feel slightly bumpy and how I could use small stroke lines to create that same texture in my drawing. As I colored my drawing, I again thought aloud about how the color green I chose really didn't show what the plant looked like because the real plant had so many shades of green within it. I then modeled how I could use a lighter touch or different colors of green to create the variation in my drawing that was present in the real plant and still let the veins be seen.

As the days progressed, students began adding details to their drawings. As the study continued, they incorporated some of the techniques I shared during the class notebook entry and their drawings became larger (see Figure 3–4) and they used labels to identify unique features of the plants (node, parallel veins). Shading techniques were used, giving the drawings depth. Students began to see how powerful drawings could be in representing their observations.

Figure 3–4. A first grader's detailed drawing of a leaf

In this vignette, the teacher conducted an "on-the-fly" assessment and made a decision to stop the lesson early to conduct a minilesson through the class notebook entry. In presenting different techniques for drawing, the teacher provided a scaffold for the students, allowing all students an opportunity to hear the thinking process behind making a quality drawing. Additionally, the class notebook provided a visual model to guide students to enhance their entries.

QUESTIONING

Students at any grade level should be able to ask questions of each other of the texts they read, the features of the phenomena they observe, and the conclusions they draw from their models or scientific investigations. (National Research Council 2012, 56)

As students work with materials, they are constantly asking questions although they might not realize it. Science notebooks become important tools for the students to capture these questions for future investigations. In the beginning, students might not be clear in recording their questions; instead, their questions are intermingled within their observations, making it difficult to distinguish them from other elements of their notebooks. Questions go unexplored and unaddressed within their work. Questions they record might not be relevant to their investigation, as the role of questions is not clear to many students at this point.

With more experiences, students progress by beginning to recognize valuable questions. They record these in a manner that sets them apart from other elements of their notebooks. Students use techniques that allow them to quickly locate their questions, such as beginning their entries with their questions, designating a specific area of their notebooks for questions, or coding their questions in some manner. At this stage, students' questions are relevant to their investigations and might be actively pursued if time is provided. There is an understanding that questions are an important part of the work of scientists and therefore an important element of science notebooks.

Over time, the questions that students raise are not only easy to find but might be organized in a meaningful manner as well. Students might begin grouping questions according to aspects of their investigations, such as behaviors or physical characteristics. Questions serve a purpose and are thoughtfully considered by the students as they revisit them from time to time, address them within their entries, and view them as starting points for new questions.

USING SCIENCE NOTEBOOKS AS A RESOURCE

Students should write accounts of their work, . . . to produce reports or posters that present their work to others. (National Research Council 2012, 77)

Science notebooks do not serve their true purpose unless students use them as resources to build scientific concepts and develop communication skills.

This is accomplished any time students refer to the information within their notebooks. For many students, referencing their notebooks helps establish a purpose for recording and organizing the information pertaining to an investigation. This can be achieved by asking students to refer to their notebooks when discussing ideas with a partner or group, such as during the content discussion within the Cycle of Notebook Interaction.

As students become more comfortable with using notebooks as a resource, they begin to reference the information within them for more formal sharing. Just as scientists present their ideas to others, students need to be encouraged to present their findings beyond their casual conversations. After a crucial point in an investigation, students might be asked to create an explanation, including a claim, evidence, and reasoning, and to argue their point during a science talk. At the end of an investigation, students might be asked to present their findings in a more formal manner, such as a science conference, slide show, informational writing piece, or big book. The importance of having pertinent, accessible information in their notebooks takes on new meaning once the investigation materials are no longer available for reference.

In the following vignette, a teacher describes how science notebooks are utilized as resources in a second-grade classroom.

See Chapter 6 for more on science talks.

> After studying the mealworm for several weeks, we had a class discussion of how we could share this information with others. One student suggested that the class could make a book. After reviewing their notebooks, the class brainstormed a list of ideas they felt should be included in the book and listed these on the board. The students decided to take a chronological approach to sharing the information and determined that the book should focus on the life cycle of the mealworm. Students broke up into groups of four, with each group focusing on a different component of the life cycle. Within the groups, students started by looking back in their notebooks for information pertaining to their stage of the life cycle. They compared notes, recording the ideas they thought to be most important on sticky notes. Finally, they shared tasks such as writing, drawing, and organizing their page of the book. At the end, we had a class big book with each page created using information from their notebooks.

In this vignette, the teacher created an authentic opportunity for the students to use their notebooks as reference tools. In creating the pages for a class big book, the students needed to go back through their notebooks and pull out the most important information. Such a process might also help students recognize the importance of recording information to go back to it later.

Progress in Developing Conceptual Understanding

What evidence of progress is there in students' conceptual understandings?

The first goal of using science notebooks is to develop and reveal student understanding of the scientific content being studied. Such development is represented within the notebook through their explanations and reflections. Just as you can support students in developing the skills necessary for documentation, you can help students focus on key science concepts—what *A Framework for K–12 Science Education* (National Research Council 2012) calls the "disciplinary core ideas."

EXPLANATIONS—CLAIMS, EVIDENCE, AND REASONING

Early in their science education, students need opportunities to engage in constructing and critiquing explanations. They should be encouraged to develop explanations of what they observe when conducting their own investigations and to evaluate their own and others' explanations for consistency with the evidence. (National Research Council 2012, 69)

The development of explanations helps students focus on the science content. As described in Chapter 2, an explanation contains a claim, evidence, and reasoning. In the beginning, explanations might not be present within the science notebooks, as students focus on capturing their observations and documenting their investigations. Students use words or pictures to include ideas about the content within their entries, such as the needs of an insect or a description of a mixture, but they do not structure their ideas in the form of an explanation. Early on, one might start to see the beginning stages of explanations with simple claims, such as "Seeds sprout," or evidence, such as "My seed is growing." At these beginning stages, claims and evidence might also

The focus question plays a key role in students' explanations. Some questions might guide students to write full explanations, and others might ask for their thinking rather than making a claim.

be present in the form of a drawing of a bag with a sprouted seed. Reasoning is more complex and is often not present within early notebook entries.

With some support from the teacher, in the form of well-thought-out focus questions and/or scaffolding of the language of claims, evidence, and reasoning, students begin to show progress with their explanations. They move from simple claims to more complex claims with a statement about their evidence, such as "Seeds need water to sprout and grow because the seed on a wet paper towel sprouted but the one on a dry paper towel did not." At this stage, students might provide multiple sources of evidence to support their claim. Students begin to incorporate reasoning at this point as well, although at this stage, they might simply repeat the ideas presented as their claim and evidence, such as "I think this happened because the one on the wet paper towel had a green sprout." It is also common to see claims and reasoning not supported by evidence, such as "Seeds sprout in water because plants need water to grow."

With experience, students are able to construct an explanation that contains all three parts. They make specific claims, use data as part of their evidence, and provide reasoning that connects their idea to the larger scientific concepts being studied. The quality and complexity of their explanations depend greatly upon the focus question they are attempting to answer. At this stage, students might produce an explanation, such as "The lima bean seeds need water to sprout. I know this because all five seeds in the bag with a moist paper towel sprouted but the ones in the bag with a dry paper towel still look the same as they did in the beginning. I think this happens because all plants need water to grow." With scaffolding students are able to formulate solid explanations that help them develop their scientific understandings.

For more on explanations and ways to scaffold student development of explanations, see Chapter 2.

This section examines how students progress in their documentation of the core ideas within their science notebooks and how this helps students develop scientific understandings.

DISCIPLINARY CORE IDEAS

An important role of science education is not to teach "all the facts" but rather to prepare students with sufficient core knowledge so that they can later acquire additional information on their own. (National Research Council 2012, 31)

As described in Chapter 1, the first goal of science notebooks is to develop understanding of the scientific content. During discussions, it is sometimes difficult to know if all students understand the idea, as some might not contribute to the conversation; however, when writing explanations students must articulate their ideas. These explanations provide insight into the student's level of understanding when looking at the science notebook for formative assessment purposes. Figures 3–5 through 3–7 demonstrate different levels of notebook entries communicating the relationship between the length of a catapult arm, the amount of potential energy, and the distance the object travels. In the beginning, students might struggle to convey

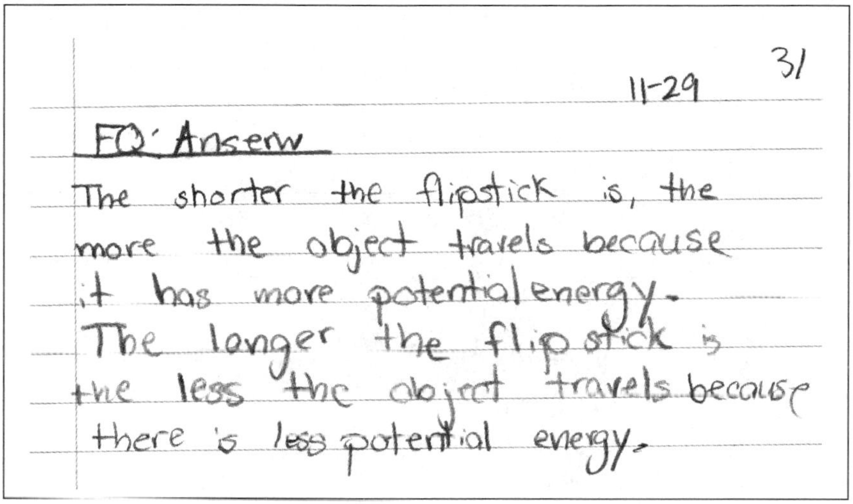
11-29 31
FQ: Ansenw
The shorter the flipstick is, the more the object travels because it has more potential energy.
The longer the flip stick is the less the object travels becaus there is less potential energy.

Figure 3–5. A student's notebook entry that demonstrates a clear understanding of the content

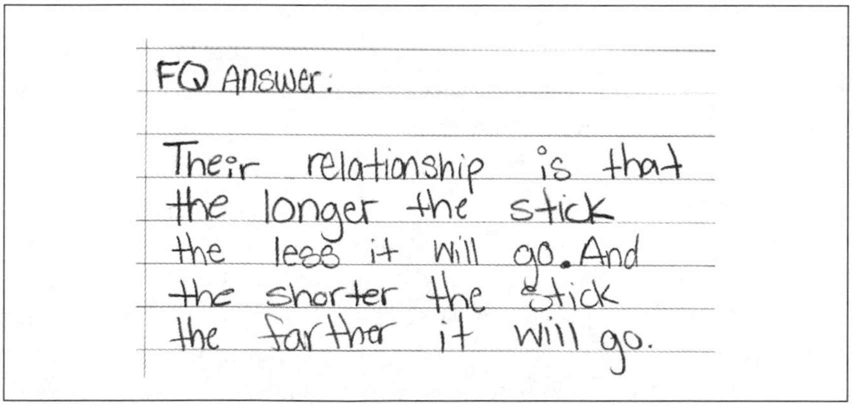
FQ Answer:
Their relationship is that the longer the stick the less it will go. And the shorter the stick the farther it will go.

Figure 3–6. A student's notebook entry that demonstrates understanding of the content, but that understanding is not communicated well

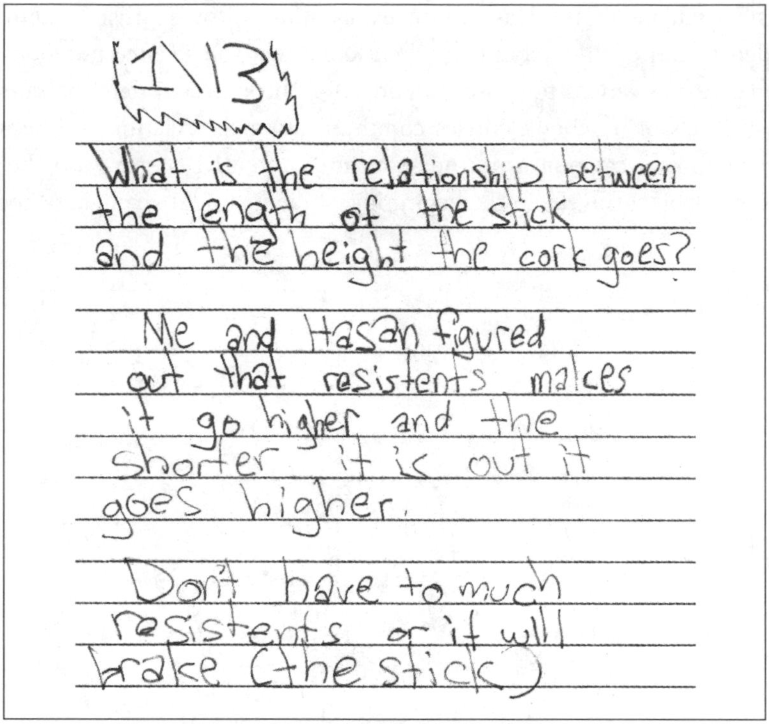

1\13

What is the relationship between the length of the stick and the height the cork goes?

Me and Hasan figured out that resistents makes it go higher and the shorter it is out it goes higher.

Don't have to much resistents or it will brake (the stick)

Figure 3–7. A student's notebook entry that demonstrates a lack of understanding of the content and beginning communication skills

For information on how to support and scaffold the development of students' entries, see Chapters 1 and 2.

their understandings in writing, even though they are able to verbalize their ideas. The appearance or length of an entry might not reflect the content that is present. Some students record very little in their notebooks or organize their information in a manner that appears to be disorganized; however, they might be able to explain the content being studied. Some students might be quite proficient writers, but upon reading their entries it becomes clear that there is a lack of understanding of the content.

Student understanding of the content should progress throughout the unit of study as they gain experience with the ideas and the related vocabulary. Within the notebook entries, these understandings move from isolated ideas about an investigation to demonstrating connections to the broader scientific ideas. With various supports and scaffolds, such as specific feedback provided on self-stick notes and sentence frames, students are able to progress and express their ideas in writing, as this vignette demonstrates.

The students had been working with solutions and had spent some time exploring physical changes. To explore chemical reactions, they mixed calcium chloride, baking soda, and water in a cup. When mixed together a reaction occurs, as evidenced by fizzing, temperature and color change, and a new substance being formed. The next day after the investigation, I asked students to review their notes from the investigation and to talk with a partner about the evidence they had collected and what type of reaction had occurred. Then, I asked students to answer the focus question, "What evidence might you find when a chemical reaction occurs?" That afternoon, I collected the notebooks to look at their responses to see how well they understood this concept. I read through each entry and sorted the notebooks into two piles according to their understanding.

1. Students who had a good understanding of the content—they described what they saw happening in the cup and related it to the new substances formed, gas and a precipitate.
2. Students who had some understanding but their ideas were incomplete—for example, they described one piece of evidence of reaction in great detail but did not mention the other pieces of evidence.

For those in group 2, I posed some questions on self-stick notes to help the students think further about the evidence they had collected during their investigation and put the notes in their notebooks. The next day, I partnered those from group 2 with students from group 1 and gave them time to talk again about the focus question and encouraged them to practice our skills of argumentation, such as agreeing/disagreeing and asking for evidence. After this discussion, I had students draw a line in their notebooks under their entry from the previous day to add new ideas. I then collected group 2's notebooks that afternoon and was happy to see that most of the students had included more than one piece of evidence and seemed to have a more complete understanding.

This vignette describes how the teacher engaged in the process of formative assessment at a critical point to ensure her students had a good understanding of chemical reactions. Based on what she learned, she modified her lesson plan for the next day to allow her students a bit more time with the concept. Having students talk with one another allowed her to move from group to group and provide some small-group instruction to those students with whom she was most concerned.

Progress in Taking Ownership of Their Science Notebook

Students are the ones who must ultimately take action to bridge the gap between where they are and where they are heading. (National Research Council 2001, 17)

What evidence is there of student progress toward ownership of the science notebook?

For students to fully realize the notebook's potential, they must reflect on the work they are doing to determine understandings and new goals. Students who are new to notebooks might require assistance to reflect upon their work and determine next steps to take. As they begin this process, students may assess themselves not by asking "Does the work show what I learned?" but rather "Does it look neat?" or "Did I finish?" Eventually, the students' assessment shifts to setting goals focused on improving the overall notebook so that it becomes a valuable tool. For example, a student might indicate that she needs to work on experimenting with different methods to organize her data or using evidence to support her claim.

As part of this process, students need time to reflect on their understandings of the core ideas and how they can use the information within their notebooks to help them make sense of the bigger scientific ideas. When students first begin to use notebooks, they might simply record information and not interpret their findings. Students might see their notebooks as collections of data that they can look through, but they do so with the purpose of reexamining facts or looking at what they did rather than trying to make sense of their thinking. As students share with a partner or a group, they focus on factual information. Students often look to the teacher for direction or confirmation that they are doing well, rather than relying on their own interpretation of their work.

As students become more experienced with science notebooks, they begin to see them as tools for making connections between what they are observing and their prior experiences. They no longer use notebooks solely for data collection; instead, they begin to synthesize their thoughts, which might include writing for several minutes after an investigation or looking over several days of work to determine connections between investigations that lead to the bigger ideas of science. As students become more reflective, they recognize both patterns and inconsistencies in their data. With the support of focus questions, students attempt to explain their thinking and begin to formulate partial explanations, such as "I think that when heavy rain falls on steep land, deep canyons will be made because the large amount of water carries the deposits away with more force."

As primary consumers of their notebooks, students continually self-assess their progress toward their goals. The students then adjust their work based upon how well they think they are meeting their goals.

> We believe it is important that students be given the opportunity and time to self-assess their work and act on that information to progress.

Notebooks are essential components to learning science and need to be developed over time. Students will approach each of the areas discussed in this chapter in very unique ways, and they will improve their skills at various rates. It is important that students recognize the uniqueness of their notebooks and view the class notebook and other students' notebooks as models rather than as means of comparison. It should be emphasized that each student's notebook is unique, and although the notebooks have similar content, they should not look identical to anyone else's. It is essential that teachers examine the notebooks at critical points in the investigation to inform instruction and provide supports and scaffolds to help the students develop their notebooks to their fullest potential. Although students' notebooks might not look perfect, they will progress with support from the teacher.

THINKING POINT: How will you gather evidence of your students' progress within each of the areas discussed in this chapter? What opportunities will you provide to allow students to improve in each of these areas so that their notebooks support learning in science?

4 Discussions with Scientists and Engineers

Scientists develop explanations using observations (evidence) and what they already know about the world (scientific knowledge). Good explanations are based on evidence from investigations. Scientists make the results of their investigations public; they describe the investigations in ways that enable others to repeat the investigation. Scientists review and ask questions about the results of other scientists' work. (National Research Council 1996, 123)

How Scientists and Engineers Use Their Notebooks

To consider authentic implementation of notebooks used by scientists and engineers, it is important to understand how notebooks are used in their line of work. We interviewed Kay Rohde, Alan Gallaspy, Trent Northen, Gilbert Magbag, and David Belasco separately, and they shared ways they have used notebooks. Kay provided insight as a national park specialist on observational fieldwork. Alan, a forensic scientist, offered information from the perspective of a controlled lab setting. Trent discussed his use of notebooks as part of a team of scientists, and Gilbert and David shared their use of notebooks in the field of engineering. We also asked the scientists and engineers to consider what is important for teachers and students to take into account when using notebooks.

Please describe your job.

Kay: I am chief of interpretation for Lake Mead National Recreation Area [in Nevada and Arizona], which means that I manage all of the information and educational services in the park. My current position does not require me to use a notebook, so I will focus on my experiences when I worked in a cave. I worked as a cave specialist for a number of years.

Alan: I am employed as a forensic scientist at one of the regional crime labs in town and usually work in the toxicology section. Toxicology is the study of the disposition and effects of poisons; most of my work is centered on drunken driving and various crimes where drugs of abuse might be involved. I also occasionally find myself testing specimens from people who have been accused in murder cases so I can better understand their thought processes at the time of the crime.

Gilbert: I am a Project Manager for a health care corporation, responsible for the implementation of a management system at the plant level.

Trent: I am a Principal Investigator in charge of an analytical chemistry lab. Our lab develops and applies new methods for a broad range of applications including helping develop biofuels, cancer diagnostics, and gaining insights into global carbon cycling.

David: I have had a number of different roles while working as an engineer at Alliant Techsystems, Inc. (ATK), and for each one I've leveraged my degree in mechanical engineering. At ATK, we design systems for the U.S. military. I have worked on projects where I am responsible for the design of components in a system; we call this working as an individual contributor. In this type of role, I make calculations and drawings to show that my designs will meet the project requirements. I've led teams of individual contributors designing a set of components for a project. At ATK, we call this a lead of an Integrated Product Team or IPT lead. I've also been responsible for entire systems where I direct work of IPT leads from several engineering disciplines like mechanical, electrical, software, and systems engineering. This role is called a Technical Director.

What type of notebook do you use in your work?

Kay: The science notebook we used had a slightly different purpose; it was actually a survey book with waterproof pages, because caves can get dripping wet. We had a staff logbook in which everyone would record cave conditions. Many of our entries would have a sketch with the actual readings: forward, backward, azimuth, the whole nine yards. We would also inventory resources. For each survey station, we would list everything around us and sketch the room. We also kept personal notebooks while leading cave tours, keeping watch of things in the cave, noting differences. Eventually, we used the information in the notebook to help us develop a picture of what a year in the cave looked like. We were able to document changes and use it as the basis of research later.

Alan: We are running the entire spectrum of notebooks these days. We may maintain a small spiral notebook as a record of small off-the-cuff calculations. Or, we may make some kind of notation that there is a leak in the roof that was dripping on one of the instruments to remind us to have it fixed.

We also maintain extensive logs. For example, if we have a piece of instrumentation or some kind of analytical device, we may keep a logbook on it detailing maintenance issues, what kind of calibrations have been performed on it over time, what kind of repairs may have been made on it, when it was placed in service, and when it was taken out of service.

We have logbooks and computer systems to help us keep track of each piece of evidence that comes in and goes out of the laboratory. We are just surrounded by paper all over the place and it can get kind of crazy at times.

Gilbert: The notebook that we generally use is called an A3. The A3 gets its name from the size of the paper that it is written/printed on, which is eleven by seventeen inches. All A3 information is contained to a single side of this paper.

Trent: We use both paper and electronic notebooks and I'm really pushing for everyone to use electronic notebooks. Even paper notebooks are digitized periodically so that they can be viewed on our internal Wiki.

David: When I work as an individual contributor or IPT lead, I use a spiral-bound notebook to hold my work. I'm still searching for an electronic format to hold all my notes and work, but I haven't found anything I like more than a notebook.

We also store project data on a server where teams can access it through the Internet. The goal is to make the data available and searchable. This data are mainly notes from meetings, presentations, calculations in software, and final reports.

What type of information do you record in your notebook and how do you organize it?

Kay: The survey book was not just my book; it was a community book. We actually taught note taking as one of the skills for working in the cave to maintain consistency in this community survey book. When you went in on a survey crew, you learned what and how to record. We had a tape person who measured and a note taker who could write legibly and take it all in. There was a real skill to note taking, not just getting the numbers down as the tape person called them out, but being able to sketch and record all the details.

For every surveying point, we had to do a physical sketch of the room, both in cross-section as well as in plain view. The survey book became a document of everything in the cave, an inventory of it. We would go into the cave and sketch rooms including pools of water, stalactites, stalagmites, and anything else we noticed. Most of the time, it was just normal stuff and we used shorthand, indicating a feature and the size of it. But if there was something unusual, we wrote it all down and described it in detail. Unusual items might be wet spots, fossils, and things like that.

I would also go into the cave with one of the entomologists when I worked at Carlsbad [Caverns National Park in New Mexico]. He would take his own notebook into the cave and note what he found and sketch the "critters" himself. We would bait traps, he would describe their location in his notebook, and then we would go back later and check the traps. He had to describe what the trap consisted of because those things could become variables in his work. When we captured insects, he would note all of the details: where the insect was found; what it looked like; conditions of the area; temperature; substrate, sometimes taking a sample of it; behavior; and time, although this might be considered irrelevant in a cave.

Alan: We spend a lot of time organizing and documenting the experiments that we are going to perform. For example, if we want to test several blood specimens for their alcohol level, there are a lot of things that we will do for that particular experiment. We will make a list of the samples that we will run for that particular experiment. For each of those samples, the unknowns, there will be demographical information. For example, each blood sample would have a name and maybe a case number associated with it. We might even have multiple samples from the same person drawn at different times, and we might have a number of different people all involved in one case. So we have to have some type of system to keep all of those things organized and not confuse one with the other.

In addition, if we are doing quantitative analysis, we want to have different information on where we obtained the quantitative calibrators: the manufacturer, lot number, and date of manufacture. We might have additional information on the lot numbers of different reagents used in a particular experiment. Those are just some of the elements of an experiment that we have to keep track of one way or another.

I was not by any means the first employee for that particular laboratory, and there were various systems in place already. I was given a certain amount of latitude to do things my own way, but nonetheless, I was expected to comply and conform to whatever systems were currently in place. There is no sense in allowing one person to reinvent the wheel. If there is something that is known to work, to fulfill the needs of that particular institution, it makes sense to go ahead and educate others about that system.

Gilbert: There are two formats of A3s that we use—Strategic and Problem Solving. Strategic A3s are business strategy related; they reflect on previous/current activities and trends and provide a strategy for moving forward. Problem Solving A3s, like the name suggests, are written to solve problems. These describe the problem, identify potential root causes, and provide solutions to address those root causes. Both types of A3s include action lists and a schedule for completion; both should be reviewed regularly to ensure progress is being made.

Although A3s are generally written by one person, they are very much a team effort. A team, its members, and any stakeholders have input into the content of the A3 and can contribute at any time. Again, these must be reviewed frequently to ensure that progress is being made.

We don't have specific protocols associated with the A3s, there are no specific formats for either of the A3 types. Generally any format will suffice if the A3 tells the complete story or paints a complete picture. We do make sure, however, to review A3s on a frequent basis, as these are living documents and need to be updated so the reader always has the most current revision of the story.

Trent: Any materials that support publications and patents. This may include very minor details and observations to make sure that we can reproduce the experiments. Essentially everything is documented in some form or another.

David: I like to have separate notebooks for separate projects, or at least different sections per project so I can record things through the life of the projects on continuous pages. When I want to reference things I've done in the past, I recall the project first so organizing my work by project makes life easier for me.

When I'm beginning a new design project, I start by recording the objectives, requirements, and assumptions that I make about the problem. Then I'll make some sketches of how I believe things will work. I might start modeling the sketches in computer software; when I do that, I'll print some pictures and paste them in my notebook. After the sketching and computer modeling, I make some notes about the calculations I will need to make to ensure the design is robust. When I think about the loads on the design I find it helpful to doodle on the sketches or drawings with the forces acting on the components. This helps me think and clarifies which calculations I must do.

Sometimes the calculations are simple enough to write down in my notebook, but there are other times when additional computer models are required. Again, I'll print and paste the summary results of the computer modeling in my notebook. Typically, after the calculation step I see something I want to improve upon so I'll do another sketch and calculation iteration loop.

After the calculations, we build prototypes to test. I'll make some notes on how I expect the design to be assembled and then adjust my notes with new ideas or changes that are made when the device is actually assembled. Even the best engineer will need to make adjustments when their product is put together for the first time. One of the most important things to document is testing. During the test I write down details on the test equip-ment and observe and note anything unexpected. In my work we typically use electronic instrumentation to record large amounts of data. After I review the data I make a summary and put that in my notebook.

After testing is completed I typically write a final report that relies heavily on the data and observations from my notebook.

How did you use the information in your notebooks?

Kay: A lot of the cave was sitting right under parking lots, and we began to notice some trends in our notes. With the notes, we knew where all the wet places were, where there was dripping or water forma-tions. Those notes provided us with data and became the begin-nings of hydrological studies. In those studies we used dye tracing to help us make sense of the trends we were seeing. We ended up finding petrochemicals in some of the water samples, and we could directly tie the information to the parking lots, and it was the notes in our survey book that began to show us the trends.

Our notes also helped us develop a picture of the cave. We would take the numbers we recorded while underground and con-nect them to numbers on the top. This allowed us to actually con-struct a map of the cave in relationship to the surface under which it lay. With surveying, we were able to check how accurate we were with our data. When we surveyed around and the walls of the cave did not meet, we knew we had some errors in our data. Knowing this allowed us to revisit data and develop an accurate picture of the cave.

Alan: We might conduct various experiments to draw a conclusion. For example, for a drunken driver, we will analyze the quantitative level of alcohol in the person's blood and we will have the sup-porting data we generated for that particular sample. Based on that quantitative level, we can say whether or not someone was perhaps under the influence of alcohol while he was driving. We're fully prepared to present those findings, as more of an adversarial courtroom presentation, at that point.

Gilbert: We always try to "paint a complete picture" on a single sheet of paper. Only the relevant information is included; anyone that has read an A3 should know all of the details about a particular issue as well as the actions to be completed, and they will know these things in the time it takes to read the entire A3, which is about five to ten minutes.

Trent: I would say that one of the big purposes of notebooks is to link an experiment to a data file and vice versa and to know what that file means. Once you get something to work, you typically go back to that and follow the same procedure; this is why it is so critical to take careful notes. Often minor details are important (e.g., which bottle of a reagent was used). It is also common that once someone in the lab works out a really good procedure, others in the lab will want to follow it, and we will use the notebook to define a standard protocol for the lab. Another important application of notebooks is recording how to use instrumentation. Recording detailed steps in your notebook is especially important if it is an instrument that you don't use every day. That's the value of the notebook; it's your own way of seeing the world and remembering it.

If we find a strange or unexpected result, we will consult our notebooks to see if there were any observations that would explain this result. We also consult our notebooks when preparing publications and patents to make sure we are including all of the appropriate details.

What role does technology play in the notebooks you keep?

Gilbert: Electronic versions of our A3s make it simple to edit and simple to share, especially in the large company in which I work. They also become searchable, making it easy to find specific A3s or information within those A3s.

Trent: We have our electronic notebooks and scanned paper notebooks on an internal website that allows me to keep track of research much more effectively than I could when I had to track down the actual paper notebook. We also include photos that are often extremely helpful in capturing experimental details.

David: In my work, technology supplements my engineering notebook. My designs are created in 3-D modeling software, and drawings to build the parts are made in that software package. Most all of my calculations are done with software. Data collected during testing are imported to spreadsheets or other modeling software to help visualize the results in graphical forms. I use a number of different technologies to support my design, but I continue to use my notebook to keep a summary of the work done in other tools.

Personally, my creative process requires sketching and annotating, and I haven't found a technology that I believe is easier or quicker than a notebook and pencil. I keep looking and trying new things with the hope that I can find an electronic replacement. As I see tablet computers get more precise and powerful, I think I'll see a crossover to an all-electronic notebook in the near future.

What role does the notebook serve in the engineering process?

Gilbert: Many times the A3 is a summary of project information, so it pulls together all of the relevant information used in the decision-making/problem-solving process. There are other documents we use that contain the information asked in the questions that ultimately feed the A3 (project plans, operation plans, technical reviews, testing protocols and their associated results documents, etc.).

David: I use my engineering notebook throughout the engineering process. One of my favorite bosses told me he thought engineers felt the need to sketch their ideas instead of just using words. That holds true for me; writing and sketching help me think about the design and the issues throughout the design, analysis, build, and test.

How do you communicate your ideas and the result of your work with others? What role does your notebook serve in that process?

Trent: Our work is shared to the general scientific community through publications, presentations, and posters. Publications should have all of the information in there to communicate what was done, what the results were, and how you interpret the results with sufficient detail such that it can be reproduced. The publication becomes its own entity, separate from the notebook. However, the notebooks typically contain more details than are included in a publication and are essential to preparing the publication.

As the scientists and engineers indicated, what they use for notebooks, what is recorded in the notebook, and how the notebook is used vary greatly. There is no established notebook that all scientists or engineers use nor is there one specific method that dictates their development. The notebook is a tool to help scientists and engineers conduct their research, answer questions, and solve problems. What is recorded, the method for recording within that notebook, and the use of technology are both purposeful and meaningful to the user.

Recommendations for the Classroom

Science notebooks are an essential component in the scientific and engineering community. Therefore, it is important to understand the perspective of scientists and engineers on why notebooks should be used in elementary classrooms. Here are what our scientists and engineers had to say about the role of notebooks in elementary science.

Why should children use science notebooks?

Kay: The main thing is to get the observations and information down; reflection will come later. If reflection is pushed too soon, it will get in the way of accurately recording the data, which is critical. In a science notebook, students should be gathering information and taking notes so they can do something with the information later, such as build a map, construct an experiment, look up something, or identify a little bird.

  I think that using the notebook will help kids be able to verbalize and describe. Recording in the notebook will help in vocabulary development and describing; being able to write descriptively is better in the long run no matter what they do.

Alan: You can never depend on your memory. I can't even remember what I had for breakfast this morning. If that was important, I should have recorded it in my notebook. But nonetheless, it would be foolhardy to rely on your memory for a particular experiment, no matter how simple it might be.

Gilbert: Notebooks are a great reference, especially with a subject like science that has so much information and many details to remember. Notebooks can provide information in an organized manner, making it easier to find.

Trent: For the same reasons that we do, to make sure all of the details and observations made during their experiments are documented such that they can refer back to them when interpreting the results.

David: Everyone involved in science fields should use a notebook of some kind because it's critically important. I am consistently telling the teams with whom I work that if an accomplishment isn't documented, we did not really accomplish anything. But if you do not write down your thoughts or how you solved the problem, how can you describe it to others or be sure you can do it again? By using notebooks and documenting the path to our successes, we solve problems faster with fewer stumbles along the way. Science notebooks are the foundation that allows you to successfully build upon your previous work.

What are the elements that you feel are essential for student notebooks?

Kay: I think that the notebook is something that builds. Background data are essential—who, what, when, where, why, and how, particularly who, when, and what because all of that influences the investigation. With young kids, it is starting small, with very simple data, such as the temperature. As students get older, they are going to figure out what else might go in there. I would probably want students to record who they are working with because that becomes important if there are questions. Then I would consider items that are specific to whatever is being investigated. Having that information helps build a picture of conditions for whatever is being done. The other thing I would want to see kids include is some questions because those are the kinds of things they go back to and say, "Hmm, let's look into that."

Alan: It is good to try to keep as much detailed and organized information as possible if you don't really know what is going to be important down the road. Completeness would account for something. You can go back from your complete notes and ascertain what was irrelevant and what was important.

Gilbert: Organization is very important; only relevant information should be included (trivia has a time and a place). Clarity is important as well—various people will be reading these, and it is essential that the information is easily understood.

Trent: The more you can get kids engaged in the question at the beginning, the better—actually trying to understand what they are doing. If they are engaged, the observations should lead to students asking their own questions, "Oh wow, is it supposed to be purple?" We all remember things differently (e.g., some of us are more visual and need to draw pictures, etc.). So it is important to give the students flexibility to capture their thoughts and observations in a way that makes sense to them.

What advice do you have about recording data and organizing them?

Kay: I hope teachers don't make kids write in complete sentences; they just need to get the ideas down. Everybody learns differently. Sometimes for me, just a word helps me remember; for others, they need more words or more descriptions. Let kids come up with the criteria that they need to record. It may be a collective class effort, but constantly do that so they learn what to record and they don't just rely on journaling. Journaling is fine, there is a place for it, but it will get in the way of the data collection, which is why scientists use notebooks—to record data. If scientists don't record the data, they can't replicate their work; they can't build a picture; they can't use the data if it is not complete.

Alan: The main take-home point is that it is good to anticipate, if you possibly can, what you want to record and then try to organize it in some sort of systematic way, be it a table, graph, or something along those lines. A little preparation goes a long way. There are, of course, different ways to record things; both in my work and in every scientific endeavor that I have been a part of in my life, there has been more than one way to record something.

For example, if students were making a series of observations of a seed sprouting, they would have to have some sort of organized, systematic way of recording those observations. They might have notebook entries ranging from the initial day—day one, day two—for as long as they care to run the experiment and make provisions for whatever observations they care to record in that particular space. But the key to these entries is to have an organized, systematic recording of the experiment.

Hopefully, students will be able to take a look at the data they generate with a known situation and apply that same experiment to an unknown situation and draw a conclusion from it. If they organize their notebooks properly, students should be able to do that.

Gilbert: Obviously not everything is included in our A3s. There are many other sources (hallway conversations, one-to-one meetings, team meetings, emails, etc.) that contribute information to the A3. It is critical that the notes from these sources are properly and accurately recorded. Again, clarity is critical. In reviewing the notes there should be no chance to misinterpret what was written. Regarding organization, there should be a flow to the information, like telling a story, to make it easy to follow and understand.

What other thoughts would you like to share?

Kay: I don't ever remember using a notebook in school. I wish that someone had taught me. I think it is important to think about how students use them so they are not considered a chore but become natural. Maybe start with just data or just observation as a first step rather than trying to do it all. To me, having to do it all would be overwhelming as a kid.

Also, I think that it has to be real; it can't be contrived. So when doing a science project, just keep notes, time, and date— these things are automatic, kind of like putting your name, class, and period on the top right corner of the paper. I think that it is a gradual thing. Sometimes there is the expectation that a third grader will automatically have the same kind of science notebook that a premed student or biologist would have. That is one of the things that teachers need to be careful of. I think that a well-developed notebook is a gradual thing.

Alan: Careful note taking is what separates science from casual observation. For instance, I have noticed for years and years that the sun comes up over the mountain. But if I wanted to quantify that a little bit better, I would have to take very systematic notes, such as exactly which part of the mountain it comes over and if I am standing in the same spot in the valley when I make this observation.

   Overall, the notebook is something that develops with time. It is like any other endeavor: you have to expose not just kids, but anyone, to a certain thing any number of times before they will get the knack of it and master it.

Trent: It can be helpful to outline the experiment before performing it to make sure you understand the experimental steps, but we don't want the experiments to become mindless. The students must be engaged in the questions. The more they can try to think through what they predict will happen and test it, the more they will learn.

David: The interesting thing I find in engineering and design is you will learn more from failures than you do from successes. When things work as expected, you get to move on to the next step, but failures cause you to stop, think, and dig deeper into the cause. The failure investigation gives you valuable experiential learning. It is important to record the steps you take to discover what went wrong in your notebook so you can leverage that in your future designs.

One of the goals in maintaining science notebooks, in addition to exploring scientific content and literacy, is to replicate the work that scientists and engineers do. These scientists and engineers have provided their perspectives on authentic use of science notebooks in different fields of scientific study. Their recommendations include: students organizing their information in a manner that allows them to access it, students understanding the purpose of the investigation, and teachers providing students with opportunities to capture their thoughts, interpret their results, and make sense of their findings.

THINKING POINT: Based upon the scientists' and engineers' perspectives, how will you make science notebooks authentic for students?

Connections to Science Education Standards

Students cannot comprehend scientific practices, nor fully appreciate the nature of scientific knowledge itself, without directly experiencing those practices for themselves. (National Research Council 2012, 30)

Connections to Science Education Standards

How do science notebooks connect to *A Framework for K–12 Science Education* and to the Next Generation Science Standards?

Science, engineering, and technology play a prevalent role in modern society. To make informed decisions and meet future challenges, all citizens need to develop an understanding of these important fields. To answer this call, experts from across the country came together to establish overarching goals for science education, resulting in *A Framework for K–12 Science Education* (National Research Council 2012), which was then used to develop the Next Generation Science Standards (NGSS) (Achieve 2013). Both documents stress the importance of engaging students in learning experiences in which they investigate the world as scientists would to gain scientific knowledge. This is accomplished by weaving three major dimensions of science learning together. Those dimensions are scientific and engineering practices, crosscutting concepts, and disciplinary core ideas, as specified in Figure 5–1.

A Framework for K–12 Science Education (National Research Council 2012) and the NGSS (Achieve 2013) approach science from the perspective that it is equally important for students to actively learn about the practices, concepts, and core ideas. The scientific and engineering practices articulate what was previously meant by the term *inquiry* and focus on the knowledge and skills students need

Scientific and Engineering Practices	Crosscutting Concepts	Disciplinary Core Ideas
1. Asking questions (for science) and defining problems (for engineering) 2. Developing and using models 3. Planning and carrying out investigations 4. Analyzing and interpreting data 5. Using mathematics and computational thinking 6. Constructing explanations (for science) and designing solutions (for engineering) 7. Engaging in argument from evidence 8. Obtaining, evaluating, and communicating information	1. Patterns 2. Cause and effect: mechanism and explanation 3. Scale, proportion, and quantity 4. Systems and system models 5. Energy and matter: flows, cycles, and conservation 6. Structure and function 7. Stability and change	**Physical Sciences** PS1: Matter and its interactions PS2: Motion and stability: forces and interactions PS3: Energy PS4: Waves and their applications in technologies for information transfer **Life Sciences** LS1: From molecules to organisms: structures and processes LS2: Ecosystems: interactions, energy, and dynamics LS3: Heredity: inheritance and variation of traits LS4: Biological evolution: unity and diversity **Earth and Space Sciences** ESS1: Earth's place in the universe ESS2: Earth's systems ESS3: Earth and human activity **Engineering, Technology, and Applications of Science** ETS1: Engineering design ETS2: Links among engineering, technology, science, and society

(National Research Council 2012, 3)

Figure 5–1 Three Dimensions of *A Framework for K–12 Science Education*

to do science. The crosscutting concepts are similar to the unifying concepts from the National Science Education Standards (National Research Council 1996) and serve as a means to make links among the disciplinary core ideas. In the past, some instruction focused only on the disciplinary core ideas of science, but the NGSS emphasize the need for all three, often picturing them as three strands of a rope intertwined together. If one strand were removed, the rope would not be as strong. As students work with the core ideas, they should engage in the practices and make connections to the crosscutting concepts, with guidance from the teacher. Science notebooks provide a means in which students can engage with the practices, crosscutting concepts, and disciplinary core ideas to construct a richer understanding of science. This chapter examines the relationship between science notebooks and the three dimensions of *A Framework for K–12 Science Education*.

Scientific and Engineering Practices

How do science notebooks help promote development of the scientific and engineering practices?

Science as practice involves doing something and learning something in such a way that the doing and the learning cannot really be separated. (National Research Council 2007, 34)

Specific notebook strategies that can be used to develop the practices are shared in Chapter 2.

The practices of science and engineering (see Figure 5–1) come from the work of scientists and engineers. They provide an outline "for students to engage in sensible versions of actual cognitive, social, and material work that scientists do" (Bell et al. 2012, 11). Students should become comfortable with these practices and use them as appropriate within their learning and to demonstrate their understandings. As students investigate, they engage in these practices, and evidence of this engagement can be found within their science notebooks. Following are examples of how each of the practices might be carried out within the science notebook.

For more information on what this evidence might look like and how it is developed, see Chapter 2.

ASKING AND DEFINING PROBLEMS: Students record findings, questions, and problems in their science notebooks. Often, questions and problems arise based on the information they have recorded. As they look back through their notebook entries, students might find that new ideas conflict with their current thinking. This conflict becomes a question and serves as a starting point for a new investigation.

DEVELOPING AND USING MODELS: Students often document their explanations of concepts using drawings or diagrams in their science notebooks. These are different from a drawn observation, as models attempt to communicate understanding of a concept. Examples might include a labeled drawing of a circuit showing the flow of electricity or a landscape showing the potential effects of a flood due to a change in the design of a runoff system. Students may also build 3-D models, such as a bridge made out of balsa wood, and put a picture of it within their science notebooks.

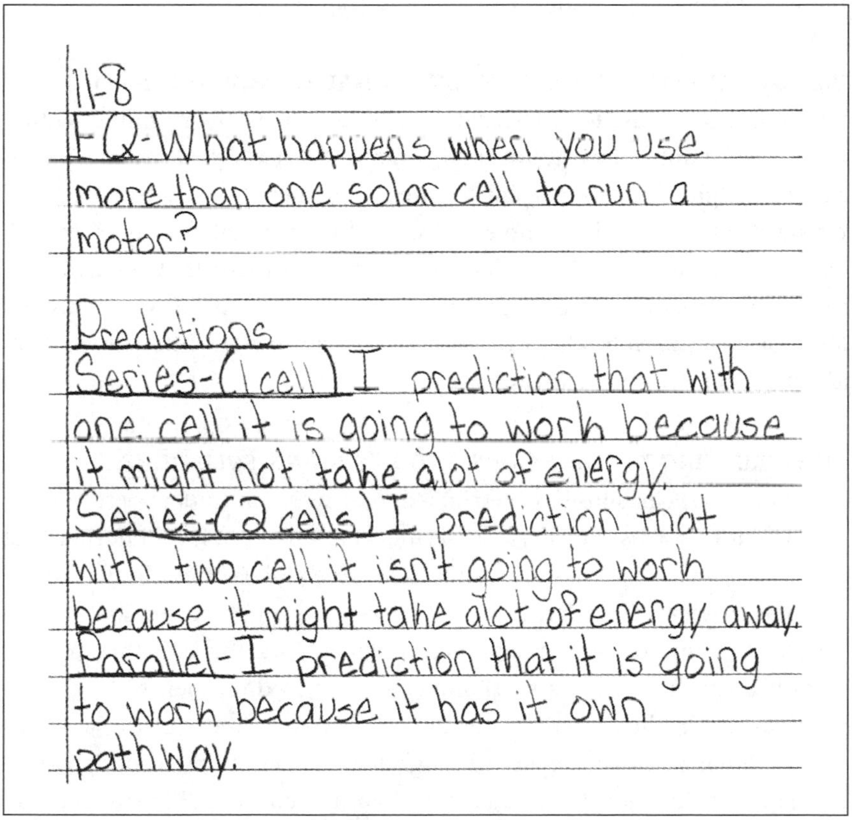

> 11-8
> FQ-What happens when you use more than one solar cell to run a motor?
>
> Predictions
> Series-(1 cell) I prediction that with one cell it is going to work because it might not take alot of energy.
> Series-(2 cells) I prediction that with two cell it isn't going to work because it might take alot of energy away.
> Parallel-I prediction that it is going to work because it has it own pathway.

Figure 5–2. A fourth grader includes predictions as part of the planning process.

PLANNING AND CARRYING OUT INVESTIGATIONS: From their questions, students plan and conduct investigations. Based on previous data, they form a hypothesis or make a prediction (see Figure 5–2), decide upon materials, and devise a way to find an answer. All of this is recorded in their notebooks, along with the work of the investigation.

ANALYZING AND INTERPRETING DATA: Data are collected in a variety of forms, including numbers, words, and drawings, within the science notebook. Students need support to put their data into useful formats, such as tables and graphs, that can help them interpret the data in a meaningful manner. Although it is sometimes helpful for students to create these tables and graphs, the teacher might provide a graph that includes labeled axes and intervals, allowing students to focus on plotting and interpreting the data rather than focusing on the creation of the graph.

USING MATHEMATICS AND COMPUTATIONAL THINKING: Students should be encouraged to use tools and numbers to document their findings within their science notebooks. Younger students might use a paper ruler to measure the height of their plant, cutting the paper ruler at the correct mark and taping it into their science notebooks, creating a visual display of growth over time that will help them calculate the amount of growth. Older students might calculate the average of multiple trials within their investigations and look for patterns within their data sets to determine how different variables affect the outcome of the investigation.

The difference between explanations, claims, evidence, and reasoning is explained in more detail in Chapter 2.

CONSTRUCTING EXPLANATIONS AND DESIGNING SOLUTIONS: The construction of explanations has been linked to increases in student performance on content-based assessments (Ruiz-Primo et al. 2010), so it is important that students include explanations within their notebook entries. Similar to developing a scientific explanation, engineers go through an iterative design process to come up with a solution. Students work through this process, from listing design criteria to refining an idea based on their tests, recording data within their science notebooks. The development of explanations and solutions can be facilitated through focused questions or design challenges that help students think deeply about the concept. The students can then reference this information as they communicate their ideas with others.

Figure 5–3 demonstrates a student's early attempt at an explanation in response to a focus question.

ENGAGING IN ARGUMENT FROM EVIDENCE: Students reference their science notebooks as they advance or defend their explanations and solutions and critically evaluate the work of their peers. They might need support in learning to use their notebooks as a reference and should be directed to look for specific information to serve as evidence from time to time. As they begin to see the value of using the notebook as one source of evidence, students will begin to document and highlight important information within their notebooks for future use. Students can also add information to their notebooks after they engage in argumentation. This refinement of their explanation might include futher clarification of their claims and reasoning as well as provide additional evidence.

OBTAINING, EVALUATING, AND COMMUNICATING INFORMATION: Throughout the investigation, students use their notebooks in discussions with others. When sufficient information has been gathered, students review their entries, weigh the merits of their data, synthesize their thoughts, and present their results to others through informal and formal written and/or oral presentations.

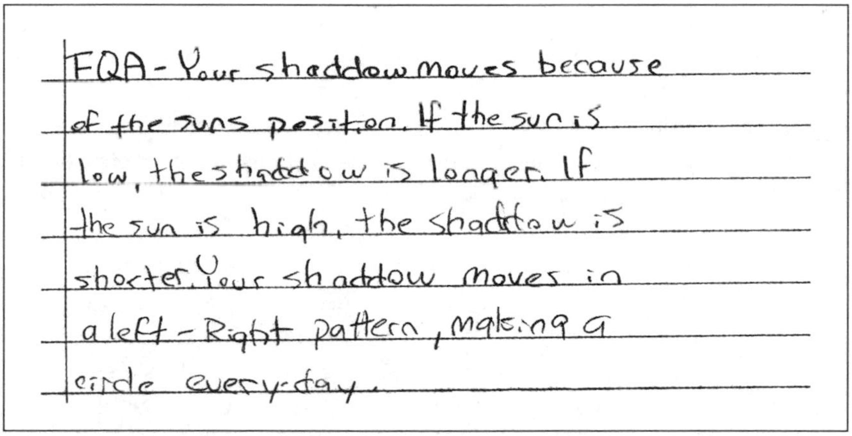

> FQA - Your shaddow moves because
> of the suns position. If the sun is
> low, the shaddow is longer. If
> the sun is high, the shaddow is
> shorter. Your shaddow moves in
> a left - Right pattern, making a
> circle every-day.

Figure 5–3. A fifth grader's early attempt at an explanation in response to a focus question

As you read the following vignette, think about which practices the students are using and how their notebooks contribute to those practices.

After exploring air resistance, students looked back through their notebooks and shared questions they had recorded while working with parachutes. I recorded these questions on the board where all the students could see them. Students then selected a question they were interested in pursuing and formed groups based on their selections. A group of three students had decided to explore how the size of the parachute affected the speed of descent.

As students began planning their investigation and developing a model for what their parachute would look like, they realized that they needed to examine the parachute they used in the original investigation, as no one knew exactly how big it was and they had nothing in their notebooks about this. After looking at their original parachutes, they decided it was a regular dinner napkin and jotted this down in their notebooks. They decided that they would cut napkins to make smaller parachutes and one person suggested that they tape some napkins together to make a really big parachute. They put these ideas down in their notebooks and then called me over. Realizing that they had not formed a hypothesis yet, I asked them what they thought would happen when they tested the parachutes. They thought the smaller parachute would descend faster and referred to the times their parachute did not open, which caused it to come down very quickly. I suggested they record this in their notebooks so they could reference it later.

The group quickly began cutting and taping napkins to make different-sized parachutes and then started testing them to see what would happen. Realizing they needed a way to organize their tests, one student suggested they name each parachute so they could write about it in their notebooks. They busily went about dropping and counting how long it took each parachute to reach the ground and recording the results in their notebooks. After testing five different-sized parachutes, one of the students commented that he didn't see much of a difference. Another student pointed out that she didn't see a big difference between each parachute, but when she looked at the results of the biggest parachute and the results of the smallest parachute, the smaller one came down faster. The students then decided to drop those two parachutes at the same time to see which one hit the ground first.

As the small groups wrapped up their investigations, I provided a focus question, "How does the size of the parachute affect the speed of descent?" to help students make sense of their data and develop an explanation based on their findings. We came back together as a whole class to share our findings. The class listened intently as each group presented their explanation and then had the opportunity to ask questions of the group. Many groups showed the parachutes they had made to the class and used evidence from their notebooks to support their findings.

In this vignette, the science notebooks played a critical role in helping students build conceptual understandings as well as engage with the practices of science and engineering. Part of doing science is documenting the work being done. The students collected their questions; planned an investigation; recognized the lack of data in previous entries; collected, analyzed, and interpreted their data; constructed an explanation with the help of a focus question provided by the teacher; and communicated their ideas to others.

Within the dimension of practices is the expectation that students learn how scientists and engineers conduct, document, and communicate their work. Students use their notebooks before, during, and after an investigation, just as scientists do. Using science notebooks in this manner helps students develop an understanding of how scientists and engineers work and the importance of this basic, yet essential, tool to their work.

THINKING POINT: What will you look for in terms of evidence of the practices of science and engineering when your students use their science notebooks?

Crosscutting Concepts

How do science notebooks help promote development of the crosscutting concepts?

The Crosscutting Concepts are the themes or concepts that bridge the engineering, physical, life, and Earth/space sciences; in this sense they represent knowledge about science or science as a way of knowing. (Duschl 2012, 11)

We provide connections to the Crosscutting Concepts without going into great detail. For more information, see *A Framework for K–12 Science Education* (National Research Council 2012).

Crosscutting concepts help students make connections between the different domains of science. These concepts (see Figure 5–1) provide a framework in which students connect the knowledge they have learned related to the various disciplines to develop a more coherent understanding. Science notebooks are authentic tools that students use to develop their understanding of the concepts presented within this dimension and bring together their science experiences.

Three of the concepts ask students to look for patterns and relationships. These include *Patterns, Cause and Effect: Mechanism and Prediction,* and *Structure and Function.* Through examining notebook entries, students begin thinking about the components of various systems and the connections that exist between them. A sense of order begins to emerge, such as identifying similarities and differences or rates of change, allowing students to bring organization to and/or raise questions about the concept with which they are working. For example, to examine patterns, students might observe the moon over a period of time, recording where they see it in the sky and its appearance. To consider cause and effect, students might use their recorded data on erosion to determine that a relationship exists between the slope of the land and the rate of erosion. After studying the structures of different insects and plants, students might sketch a model of a hypothetical insect in their notebooks to demonstrate how a particular structure functions to pollinate a plant. Students might also represent cause and effect or patterns as part of an explanation or questions for further study within their notebooks.

The crosscutting concept *Scale, Proportion, and Quantity* focuses on mathematical relationships (see Figure 5–4). Notebooks allow students to keep track of measurements and determine what would be considered appropriate data based on past experiences. By keeping notebooks, students are able to look at an object through various stages of an inquiry and note

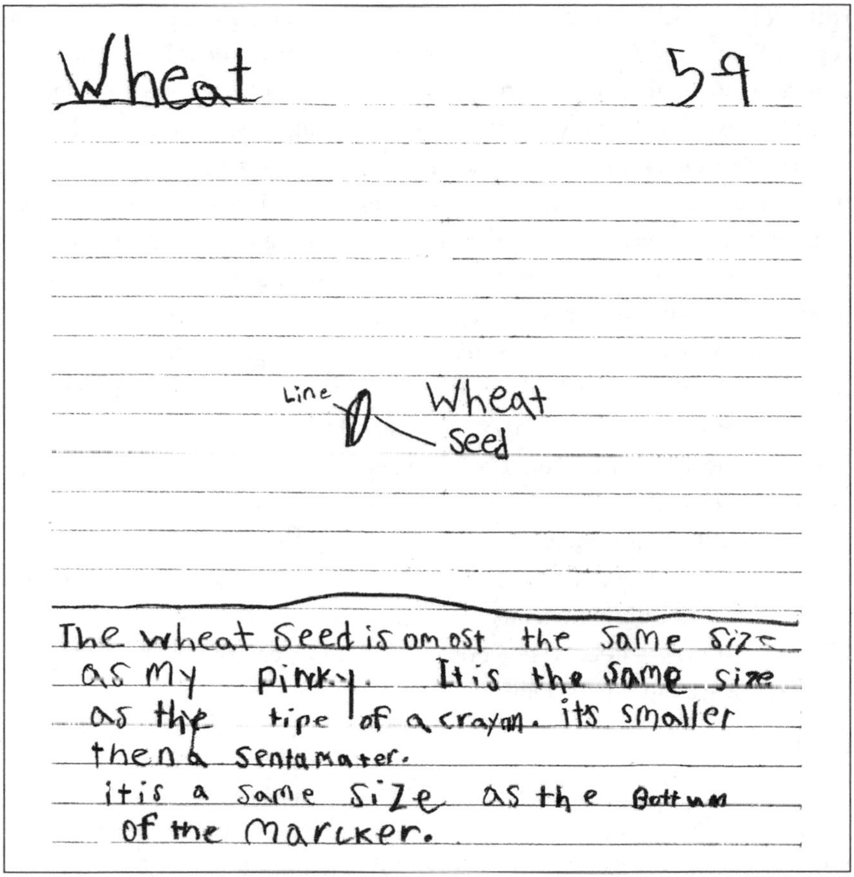

Figure 5–4. A first grader uses a ruler to measure her seed and then makes size comparisons to more familiar objects.

changes that take place or aspects that remain constant. Notebooks provide students with a quick and easy means to access information collected over time, allowing them to begin to make sense of the use of measurement and how this can help them understand phenomena.

The remaining crosscutting concepts focus on systems. First, the concept of *Systems and System Models* provides students with a way in which to study a phenomenon in small investigable components to understand the whole or to examine the roles the parts play within that system. After studying an environment, students might develop a model within their science notebooks to demonstrate the impact a drought would have on the environment, from which they could make a claim and develop an argument. Second, the concept of *Energy and Matter: Flows, Cycles, and Conservation* describes how energy flows through a system. Students might use their diagram of an electric circuit to explain the movement of energy through the system. Finally, the concept of *Stability and Change* describes the way in which a system functions. Students might set up a table to compare the impact of various solutions aimed at preventing natural events from changing the shape of the land.

It is through their written reflections and discussions that students begin to make sense of these crosscutting concepts and make connections across the disciplinary core ideas. As students write explanations, the crosscutting concepts might form the basis for their reasoning, helping them build connections between the disciplinary core ideas. However, such connections do not always occur naturally and teachers need to structure opportunities, such as those described in Chapters 1 and 2, for students to make the connections intended within this dimension.

In the following vignette, a teacher describes how first graders used their notebooks in examining balance through simple systems. As you read, pay attention to how students' notebooks help them explore the crosscutting concepts of systems and stability.

My students were exploring balanced systems using basic materials—cardboard cutouts, craft sticks as the balance point, and clothespins as counterweights. I knew my students would struggle with representing this three-dimensional system in their two-dimensional notebooks, so at an appropriate time, I modeled how to draw a diagram of the system within the class notebook—pointing out how I could represent the balance point as a rectangle within my system (see Figure 1–4 in Chapter 1). I sent students back to examine their notebook entries and make adjustments as needed to clearly represent their balanced systems.

The next day, I challenged my students to create a balanced system using a craft stick, pencil, wire, and clothespins. The pencil was to balance on its sharpened tip on the end of the craft stick. From past experiences, they knew that the clothespins, or counterweights, could be used to make an object balance. I saw some students look back at their notes to see how they had balanced the cardboard figures, and others started immediately with the materials. Soon all of them were wrapping the wire around the pencil and attaching the clothespins at various points to see if they could get the pencil to balance. As some students began creating the balanced system, other students observed what they were doing and it wasn't long before everyone had managed to create a balanced system. I gave them a few minutes to make sure they had recorded their systems in their notebooks before calling them to the floor for a group discussion. We examined the various systems they had created. I posed questions related to the location of the counterweights and the patterns they noticed about the placement of the counterweights. They quickly recognized that the counterweights needed to be lower in the system to allow it to function in a stable manner. I wanted students to think about the systems and how important each part was to the system.

At that point, I sent the students back to their seats and posed the focus question of "What is common between all of the balanced systems?" and provided a sentence frame of "All of the balanced systems _____. The systems were stable because _____" to help guide the development of their explanation within their science notebook.

In this vignette, students examined previous entries to look for patterns within their diagrams to determine how the parts of the system worked best together. They went on to explore the concept of cause and effect by setting up their system and placing the counterweights in various positions to determine the outcomes, recording those that worked and those that did not within their notebooks. Finally, in answering the focus question students communicated their understandings of their balanced systems.

THINKING POINT: How will you look for evidence that your students are using the crosscutting concepts when they use their science notebooks?

Disciplinary Core Ideas

How do science notebooks help promote the learning of physical, life, and Earth and space sciences and engineering, technology, and applications of science?

Record keeping is an important component of scientific investigation in general, and of self-directed experimental tasks especially, because access to and consulting of cumulative records are often important in interpreting evidence. (National Research Council 2007, 136)

The disciplinary core ideas refer to the information students study within physical, life, and Earth and space sciences. By using notebooks in documentation, discussion, and reflection, students begin to focus on the scientific content they know as well as how they know it—an important step in developing students' metacognitive thinking. Students begin constructing their understandings of scientific ideas as they determine what information needs to be recorded in their notebooks and the best way to organize it. As discussed in the Cycle of Notebook Interaction in Chapter 1, there are specific points at which the class comes together to discuss aspects of the investigation and the notebook. It is during these discussions that the teacher is able to turn the students' focus toward the disciplinary core ideas. Students also question one another's thinking, causing them to refer back to the evidence they collected in their notebooks to support their ideas. Reflection provides students with time to focus and write about the content they are learning, to develop their explanations, and to construct possible arguments. In reflecting on what happened and why it happened, students are developing conceptual understanding of the core ideas. The notebook itself does not develop core ideas, it is the process of writing about these ideas within the notebook that helps students develop understandings related to the disciplinary core ideas (Keys 1999; Reeves 2000; Rivard 1994; Yore, Bisanz, and Hand 2003). Notebooks provide students with one context for writing within the content of science and might be used as a tool to create other forms of informational and narrative writing. Chapter 6 provides more information on other forms of informational writing that might come from science notebooks.

The notebooks become tools for students to help explain their thinking and justify their ideas using the evidence gathered. As students work through an investigation, they begin to make connections to prior experiences. Their notebooks become reference tools during discussions as they refer to the books to find evidence to support their thinking.

In the following vignette, the teacher describes how fourth-grade students came to an understanding of disciplinary content around the pitch of sounds. How do you see them using their notebooks as part of that process of understanding?

We describe the content discussion in more detail in Chapter 1.

The students had been exploring pitch for some time and had several different experiences that allowed them to think about the connection between pitch and length of an item, such as metal bars or hollow tubes. Students were struggling with one of the investigations, a water xylophone, consisting of glass bottles with various amounts of water that needed to be put in order from highest to lowest pitch. I called the students to the floor to discuss this particular investigation. Students began by sharing their ideas with a partner before sharing them with the group. The first student to share with the group explained that the bottles needed to go in order from the least amount of water to the greatest and showed a picture he had drawn in his notebook to represent this. He went on to explain that the one with the most water had the highest pitch. Another student quickly disagreed and said she thought that the bottle with the smallest amount of water had the highest pitch.

To explore this further, we pulled the bottles out to demonstrate. The two students took turns tapping the bottles and the class agreed that each one seemed to be correct. How could this be? Another student started searching through his notebook. "I found that shorter items usually have a higher pitch, so I think the bottle with less water should have a higher pitch. This is so confusing." Students were quick to join the discussion, referring to evidence in their notebooks to support their thinking.

I listened to the conversation and realized that students had a good understanding of pitch and length, as evident by their discussion, but were getting confused with the water xylophone. From the demonstration, I realized that the two students were tapping the bottles at different locations, one above the water line and the other below. This would affect the pitch. Rather than telling students the answer, I decided to leave the water xylophone out for further investigation. We would revisit this conversation after they had more time to work with the water xylophone.

In this vignette, students made sense of the concept of pitch by looking back at their notebooks and demonstrating their ideas using the materials. Allowing time for students to talk to one another is essential to the content discussion within the Cycle of Notebook Interaction and students' sense making.

Observing how students use their notebooks during an investigation and discussion can provide insight into student understanding of the content being studied, serving as a means of formative assessment for the teacher. Notebooks represent the path of student knowledge—where they began and where they are currently.

We discuss formative assessment in more detail in Chapter 3.

How do science notebooks help promote the learning of engineering, technology, and applications of science?

This disciplinary core idea addresses how science is used to develop useful products and solutions to problems. At the elementary level, a main component of this core idea is the engineering design process. The science notebook becomes a place where students make sketches and diagrams of their ideas (much like the engineers described in Chapter 4). They consult their notebook as their sketch becomes a model to ensure that the design is properly followed. Then as they test their models, they record their data and use them to determine which design provides the best solution. As they work through the process, students communicate with one another on a regular basis, referring to their notebooks as they discuss solutions to improve upon their designs.

In the following vignette, the teacher describes how kindergartners solved a design problem. Note how they used their notebooks as they sketched out a solution, built a model, tested their solution, and presented their evidence to the class in the form of an argument.

The students planted a garden, but noticed that many of their plants were dying and the leaves had brown spots on them, as though they had been burned by the Sun. The students documented this in their notebooks through photos and drawings with captions. I recorded it in our class notebook as well, transcribing the students' ideas into words and identifying them with their names. A suggestion was made that the Sun might be too hot for the plants and perhaps the plants needed some protection from it. The students thought about this and decided we could set up a shade structure to protect the plants, much like the shade structure that protected the playground equipment. The class brainstormed a variety of materials they might use to provide shade and I recorded the list in our class notebook, which included: umbrellas, plastic, cloth, screen, tents, and so on.

I sent students back to their seats and put materials in front of them that they could use to think about what their structure might look like and begin to construct a model. After working for a while, we took pictures of their models to glue into their notebooks. I gathered everyone on the floor and asked students to share their models and why they thought they would provide shade to the plants. As students shared, I made notes of their ideas and began to mentally group students (i.e., umbrella-like structures, tent structures, canopies, etc.). To end our session, I recorded some big ideas that emerged, including *the material should block the light* and *the structure needs to be high enough for the plant to grow*, thinking aloud as I did, so the students could connect where these ideas were coming from.

The next day, we started on the floor, reviewing the ideas in the class notebook. I organized the students into groups according to the ideas they had presented. Their goal was to use their models to come up with one design to share with the group. The students spent the rest of that day making a group model and ended by sharing their new model with the larger group. Students asked questions of each group and made suggestions for changes.

Each group set out to build a model of their design that would be placed in a section of the garden to test and evaluate the design. Once the models were complete, they were set up in the garden.

Students monitored the growth of the plants within their shade structure for two weeks, recording the height and condition of the plants as well as the condition of the shade structure within their science notebooks. I compiled these data in the class notebook as well, organizing them in a table so we could compare the different structures and analyze the results. We then discussed the benefits and drawbacks to each design. Some designs were ruled out, as the plants did not fare well or the structure could not withstand the elements. Next, we developed an explanation containing a claim of which structures were the best, supported by the evidence we had collected. Students considered the designs that worked best, and each group worked to incorporate elements of those designs into new small models that they presented to the class, sharing how they had incorporated the best aspects of the previous designs. We went through a similar process again, building and testing models and making arguments. Based on the evidence presented, we selected a final solution and a large shade structure was built for the garden.

Just as with the other disciplinary core ideas, observing how students use their science notebooks during an investigation and discussion can provide insight into student understanding of the engineering design process and applications of science. Students develop this understanding as they work with others to design sketches and models within their notebooks, as they collect and evaluate data to determine if their solution meets criteria, and as they communicate their ideas with others both in written and oral forms.

Again, the notebooks are tools students use to help explain their thinking and justify their solutions using the evidence gathered. During the discussions, their notebooks serve as reference tools, as they search for and use evidence to convince others that their design is the best solution.

THINKING POINT: How will you look for evidence of understanding of the core ideas when your students use their science notebooks?

The NGSS (Achieve 2013) and *A Framework for K–12 Science Education* (National Research Council 2012) put forth a vision of students actively engaged in science and engineering investigations to develop a critical stance toward scientific ideas. Science notebooks are a natural component of this process, as pointed out throughout this chapter. However, students need support and scaffolding to use science notebooks in the manner described. Notebooks are essential tools for scientists and therefore need to be considered essential to the learning of elementary science. Notebooks help students make connections to the larger scientific concepts that they will build on throughout the rest of their education while developing literacy skills, which will be addressed next in Chapter 6.

See Chapter 1 for more on the role of the teacher in developing notebook use.

THINKING POINT: What role will notebooks play as you help students develop an understanding of the practices, crosscutting concepts, and core ideas of science and engineering?

Literacy Connections

Scientists talk through problems in real time—through publication and through less formal written venues, such as lab books, email exchanges, and colloquia. They engage in an iterative process of argumentation, model building, and refinement. . . . Just like scientists, students ask questions, talk and write about problems, argue, build models, design and conduct investigations, and come to more nuanced and empirically valid understandings of natural phenomena. (National Research Council 2007, 264)

Connections to Literacy

Experiences provide a foundation for students to develop language; by engaging students in inquiry-based science and using science notebooks, teachers are supporting this development. Besides building scientific content and replicating the work that scientists do, great potential exists for notebooks to support the development of literacy through reading, writing, and speaking.

How do science notebooks promote literacy?

Literacy instruction has changed recently largely due to the development and adoption of the Common Core State Standards for English Language Arts & Literacy in History/Social Studies, Science, and Technical Subjects (CCSS for ELA) (National Governors Association Center for Best Practices, Council of Chief State School Officers [NGA Center & CCSSO] 2010). Being literate now means students must demonstrate independence using literacy skills, build strong content knowledge, and respond to the varying demands of audience, task, purpose, and discipline. Students comprehend as well as critique, value evidence, use technology and digital media strategically and capably, and understand other perspectives and cultures (NGA Center & CCSSO 2010). Identified within the CCSS for ELA are standards for reading, writing, speaking and listening, and language designed to prepare students to be career and college ready. This chapter focuses on the third goal of science notebook use, to exercise and develop the skills of speaking and listening, writing, reading, and language use.

In the following vignette, a teacher explains how second-grade students used literacy skills as they developed an explanation and argued their ideas about matter. What skills do you notice students using as they discuss the science concepts and refer to their notebooks?

Students worked with solids and liquids in previous lessons determining the properties of both states of matter. I had students bring their notebooks to the sharing circle. Students individually reviewed the properties of solids and liquids by referring to their notebooks, and then we discussed the properties of each. The class came to consensus on solids being matter that holds its shape and can make a pile and liquids being matter that pours and takes the shape of the container. I introduced a new material, toothpaste, for students to explore and determine whether the substance was a solid or a liquid. Students recorded the focus question in their notebook and began examining the toothpaste and recording observations in their notebook. They discussed in their groups the properties of toothpaste. After students made their observations, they were called back to the sharing circle. I asked students to work with a partner to decide if toothpaste was a solid or a liquid and to use evidence to support their claim. Students worked together to construct their argument using the information from their notebook. Students shared their thinking with each other, with some indicating that toothpaste kept its shape when placed on a table like other solids. Others shared that toothpaste would pour when placed in a cup and turned upside down, like a liquid. During this time, I asked students to clarify their thinking or provide additional evidence based on their observations. Students asked each other questions in an effort to answer the focus question, "Is toothpaste a solid or a liquid?" Finally, the class discussed that toothpaste had some properties of solids and some of liquids, and students independently answered the focus question in their notebooks, providing evidence to support their thinking.

Speaking and Listening

"Oral language development precedes and is the foundation for written language development; in other words, oral language is primary and written language builds on it" (NGA Center & CCSSO 2010, Appendix A, 26). For some students, talk is an essential precursor to writing in their science notebooks. Providing opportunities for talk assists all students in feeling more secure, and as students feel secure in their thinking, they might be more open to recording their ideas in their notebooks.

How do science notebooks promote speaking and listening?

Throughout science investigations and within the Cycle of Notebook Interaction described in Chapter 1, students are encouraged to discuss ideas with partners (see Figure 6–1), in small groups, and/or with the entire class much as scientists talk to each other about their work. Some students, and perhaps some scientists, might even engage in self-talk when confronted with a difficult concept. Through this self-talk, students explore, make predictions, and analyze their work. Initially, putting ideas down in black and white might be intimidating for some students who are exploring new concepts, as writing adds a dimension of permanence. Talk, on the other hand, feels safer because ideas are discussed but are not permanently recorded. "Since talk assists learning, teachers must maximize talk opportunities for children" (Fullerton 1995, 16). As students explore with materials and begin to make observations, they talk informally as they manipulate objects, examine organisms, or design new systems. As discussed

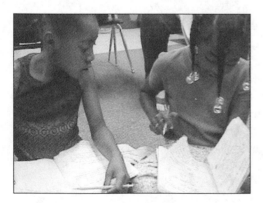

Figure 6–1. Two students discuss science concepts using their science notebooks.

in earlier chapters, with some guidance students transform their internal monologues and external dialogues into notebook entries, including drawings, narratives, or charts.

After exploration and data collection students engage in a more formal discussion. It is best to gather students in an area away from the materials and to have students sit in a circle with their notebooks in their laps or on the floor in front of them for formal discussions. This formal content discussion, or science talk, might be about the observations students are making, questions they have, or thoughts on particular concepts. Students begin by taking a moment to review their notebook entries individually. Any number of discussion protocols might be implemented to meet the specific goal of the content discussion, such as think-pair-share, to engage students in speaking and listening. Students reference their notebooks, sharing their tables, charts, or other entries as evidence to support their thinking. In the vignette at the beginning of this chapter, the teacher facilitated a discussion on whether toothpaste was a solid or liquid, as it is talk that helps students "bridge new concepts and clarify thought" (Fullerton 1995, 16). Often, it is in sharing their evidence with others during the content discussion that students begin to make sense of a concept and connect information in their notebooks to bigger ideas. Discussions using their notebooks allow them to make sense of their thinking, share their ideas with others, and receive feedback.

> We refer to the formal discussion as the content discussion part of the Cycle of Notebook Interaction described in Chapter 1.

THINKING POINT: How will you incorporate content discussions in your classroom?

Written Communication

Scientists use writing to create permanent records to establish their priority for discoveries and as documented sources for reflection, analysis, and evaluation. (Yore et al. 2006, 113)

How do science notebooks help promote written communication during science investigations?

As scientists work, they record information in their science notebooks so they are able to recall not only their data but their process for collecting data, their thinking, and their questions. The use of notebooks provides students with an authentic reason to write and synthesize their thinking to share it with others. Writing during a hands-on science investigation allows students to reflect on an experience with which they are familiar as well as aids their development of scientific concepts.

For some students, documenting their ideas while working is a difficult task. The excitement of an investigation might make it difficult for some to stop and record in their notebooks; however, it is essential that they work toward being able to do this. Recording during an investigation takes practice and requires support. Here are some simple strategies that teachers can use to support students, including English language learners (ELLs), as they write in their notebooks during the investigation. Chapter 1 shares additional strategies.

- Model recording in a class notebook using a think-aloud. The teacher verbalizes the thought process that students might have, such as, "The length of the silkworm is almost five centimeters, and it is gray with black lines, so when I record this information in my notebook, I need to describe the length of the silkworm, the color, and any other important details."
- Provide sentence stems or starters, such as, "I observe _____. This system is different because _____."
- Model technical drawings as described in Chapter 2. As students share observations, model how to record those in a class notebook.

As the year progresses and you implement strategies suggested here and in the first few chapters, recording while they work becomes second nature for the students.

Students might feel that they need to record in complete sentences; however, it might be easier to capture science observations and data with phrases and lists rather than complete sentences. Encourage various recording methods that allow students to capture the essence of the science. The primary goal of using science notebooks is to build a deeper understanding of science content; it is important that this remains the goal and that writing elements (punctuation, grammar, etc.) do not get in the way of this learning.

By using notebooks and the Cycle of Notebook Interaction on a regular basis with specific goals, students should become comfortable documenting and using various recording strategies during science investigations.

Eventually, students will be able to select a recording strategy that works best for the data they are gathering, whether that method is pictures, lists, phrases, graphs, tables, or sentences.

THINKING POINT: How will you promote writing in science notebooks during an investigation?

How do science notebooks help promote written communication after the science investigation?

In science, students make claims in the form of statements or conclusions that answer questions or address problems. Using data in a scientifically acceptable form, students marshal evidence and draw on their understanding of scientific concepts to argue in support of their claims. (NGA Center & CCSSO 2010, Appendix A, 23)

Throughout an investigation, students might reflect on their work, examine their evidence, and write about their ideas to clarify their thinking. Typically after the content discussion in the Cycle of Notebook Interaction, students are asked to make more formal claims and provide evidence about the question guiding their investigation. These initial claims and evidence serve as an opportunity for students to communicate their understanding of science concepts as well as use reasoning skills while referencing relevant evidence from their notebook.

As we explain in Chapter 3, these claims and evidence provide insight into student learning and are valuable formative assessment tools for the teacher.

After making initial claims and receiving feedback from peers and the teacher, students can extend their scientific work. Scientists frequently publish their work in a formal manner for peer review. As a goal of science notebooks is to replicate the work of scientists, students should be asked to produce final products. For students, this work can enter the writing process during literacy time and be expanded to create products (writing, slide shows, posters, oral presentations). These products provide students with an authentic opportunity to practice narrative and informational or explanatory writing; therefore, the focus of scientific products should be on sharing the information in a nonfiction format.

NARRATIVES Frequently, narratives consist of personal narratives, vivid recounts of trips to the art museum or racing around the playground. Many

Chapter 4 describes the documentation of the work of scientists and engineers.

of these narratives enter into the writing process and are edited, revised, and crafted over the course of several hours into a polished piece of writing containing strong verbs, descriptive adjectives, and adverbs. Fortunately, the CCSS for ELA (NGA Center & CCSSO 2010) places emphasis on writing about science. "In science, students write narrative descriptions of the step-by-step procedures they follow in their investigations so that others can replicate their procedures and (perhaps) reach the same results" (Appendix A, 23). A crucial piece of scientists' work is to document the methods of their experiment in their notebook.

Students' notebook entries describing their experimental setup and data collection methods serve as the beginning of these narrative descriptions. In a manner similar to the personal narrative, the procedural writing from the notebook can enter the writing process, during a designated writing time, and be edited, revised, and crafted into pieces of writing so other scientists could replicate students' work. The teacher can use specific formal writing strategies (such as minilessons on how to edit for punctuation, for example) during this time to help ELL students and others sequence their writing and use appropriate grammar and other writing conventions.

INFORMATIONAL AND EXPOSITORY WRITING Claims and evidence made after the investigation can be crafted into informational or explanatory writing as well. According to the CCSS for ELA (NGA Center & CCSSO 2010), "Informational/explanatory writing conveys information accurately. This kind of writing serves one or more closely related purposes: to increase readers' knowledge of a subject, to help readers better understand a procedure or process, or to provide readers with an enhanced comprehension of a concept . . . [Additionally, to] produce this kind of writing, students draw from what they already know and from primary and secondary sources" (Appendix A, 23). The research for this type of writing begins with students actively investigating the concept with materials and recording observations, thinking, and additional questions in their notebooks. When students are asked to produce a formal piece of informational writing, students refer to the information collected during their investigation to refine their understanding of the science content.

We recommend focusing on appropriate content from your state science standards and the Next Generation Science Standards (as described in Chapter 5).

The research is extended by reading books, visiting websites, and working further with the materials. The process of gathering information from additional sources and entering it into the notebook is explained in the reading section of this chapter. When the information is collected and organized in the notebook, students use it to make a first draft of their informational writing piece. Similar to the narrative writing, this draft can enter into the writing process, during writing time; receive feedback; and be revised, edited, and eventually published.

COMMUNICATING SCIENTIFIC WORK Often scientists and engineers are asked to make formal presentations about their work to other scientists, funding organizations, or peer groups. Students can make similar presentations, such as a status update on a design challenge, a summary of findings at the end of an investigation, or a big book to share with their peers. Science conferences are formal opportunities for students to present and justify their understandings to other students or adults. They allow students to practice the skills of writing, speaking, and listening in the context of science. The notebook serves as a valuable reference tool to prepare for and organize information for these presentations. During these presentations, students might present their explanations or arguments about scientific concepts or decisions about their designs. Explanations and arguments are an integral part of both language arts and science. According to CCSS for ELA (NGA Center & CCSSO 2010), "Although information is provided in both arguments and explanations, the two types of writing have different aims. Arguments seek to make people believe that something is true or to persuade people to change their beliefs or behavior. Explanations, on the other hand, start with the assumption of truthfulness and answer questions about why or how. Their aim is to make the reader understand rather than to persuade him or her to accept a certain point of view. In short, arguments are used for persuasion and explanations for clarification" (23).

Students can prepare to engage in argumentation, prior to making presentations, by looking at their explanations, which include claims, evidence, and reasons found in their notebooks. They consider what information supports their argument and consider what critiques might be made of their argument.

THINKING POINT: How will students formalize the information in their science notebooks to share it with a broader community?

Reading

How do science notebooks help promote reading?

Students who had more opportunities to read and write real-world informational text for purposes that went beyond just learning to read and write showed higher growth in informational comprehension and writing than those who were offered more school-only kinds of text and activities. (Duke 2010, 69)

Science notebooks serve as another tool the teacher has in promoting informational literacy among students, as the data and evidence students are using to support their arguments fits this category. Initially, student-generated writing can be a powerful motivator for beginning readers or ELLs, as it is their language and therefore highly readable. By asking students to reread their notebook entries, the teacher is encouraging them to work with informational text at their level.

After using notebooks as a beginning stage of reading, students can progress to other related informational text. After an investigation, students use other printed information for various reasons. One reason might be to verify their findings and compare those to the claims and arguments presented by others. The data recorded within the notebook, the content discussion, and the specific claims made about topics serve as a basis for comparison when students access additional texts. When reading, students determine what the text states and make inferences. They evaluate the claims made within the text by comparing them to their own knowledge, gained through firsthand experiences and recorded in their notebooks.

In the vignette that follows, note how a group of second-grade students used their experiences as a basis for the critical examination of a text.

> After several days of working with solids, students created and recorded a working definition for the term *solid*, which became part of our class word bank. They defined a solid as an object that can hold its shape without a container and can be piled. During reading, I introduced books about solids based upon the work students had done in science. As students read these books during our independent reading time, they were engaged, looking at what others said about

solids. One of the students came to me with a book in his hand and a puzzled look on his face.

"This book's definition for a solid is different than what we said."

"Why do you say that?"

"It says that a solid is a hard object. I know that feathers and fabrics are solid objects, but they don't fit this definition."

This student was using his experiences in class to think critically about the material he was now reading.

Another reason to read is to research questions that students were unable to answer through their investigations, as some questions lend themselves more to research than to inquiry. Based on their reading, students might choose to add information, in the form of direct quotes, or write a summary of what they read in their notebooks.

As you read the next vignette (from a class of third graders), think about how these students build on their work with notebooks as they use literature to help them answer their research questions.

Throughout the investigation of crayfish, students recorded questions in their notebooks. Some of these pertained to information they wanted to know but that would be difficult to investigate in a classroom setting. As the investigation started coming to an end, we looked back at our questions and determined which ones we had not found answers to at this point. Some of their questions included: "What is the natural habitat like?" "What do crayfish eat in their natural habitat?" and "How are the crayfish able to regenerate their claws?" I suggested that other scientists had studied crayfish, too, and we might refer to what they learned to help us answer these questions. I introduced a variety of books on crayfish and other crustaceans. As students read and found answers to their questions, they added this information to their notebooks.

Finally, printed materials might also be used to raise new questions. After an investigation, students are prepared to be critical readers because they are, to some degree, now experts themselves. They question text rather than accept everything they see in print. This questioning might motivate students to return to the materials to investigate ideas about which they read but of which they are not entirely convinced.

THINKING POINT: What opportunities can you provide for students to connect their notebooks to reading?

Vocabulary Development

Language is best acquired within functional contexts. . . . Students learn language not in abstract, decontextualized terms but in application, in a context that language is really for. For students, language learning occurs best when the learning context matches the real functional context. Scholars from a range of theoretical and pedagogical orientations agree that authentic experience is essential to genre and discourse learning. (Duke et al. 2006, 345)

What is the role of science notebooks in vocabulary development?

As students begin writing in their notebooks, they use language with which they are familiar to describe the work they are doing. Throughout the investigation, the students' informal language is connected to the formal scientific vocabulary by both the teacher and other students. For ELLs, "the work first focuses on discussion of scientific concepts in everyday English and then provides instructional scaffolds to help students convert the concepts into scientific language" (Lee, Quinn, and Valdés 2013, 226). Word cards, developed by teachers or students, can be hung on a word wall or placed in baskets at tables for students to access when needed. Some students might naturally record vocabulary in their notebooks and others might need prompting or a higher level of support to incorporate it. As students continue to work through an investigation, you can prompt them to dig deeper into the meaning of a domain-specific word, such as *condensation*, by asking them to discuss the meaning of the word with a partner and then engaging the class in argumentation to clarify what condensation is and what it is not. If students need further prompting, they can be asked to explain the meaning of condensation within their notebooks. You can also provide a sentence starter for students to use if needed.

Younger students can be encouraged to include vocabulary through labeled diagrams, as demonstrated in Figures 6–2 and 6–3. Other strategies can further the meaning of domain-specific words during language arts time, such as creating word cards with a student-generated drawing and sentence describing the meaning. Students can synthesize that work and insert a coherent notebook entry describing the word.

The notebook provides students with an opportunity to use vocabulary in context. Notebooks should not become a place where students copy vocabulary words along with their definitions. This does little to demonstrate how well they understand the words; rather, it demonstrates how well they can copy. Students should enter vocabulary within the context of their work in a manner that is meaningful to them.

The true potential of science notebooks will be realized when teachers provide "students with opportunities to read, write, and speak as scientists; attaching purpose to the use of print materials; and making the conventions

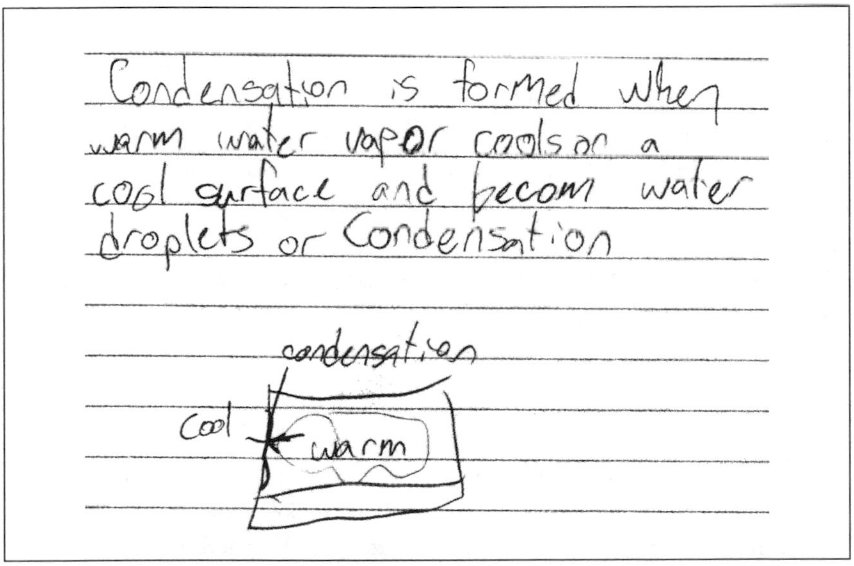

Figure 6–2. A fourth-grade student demonstrates understanding of vocabulary by embedding it in her notebook entry.

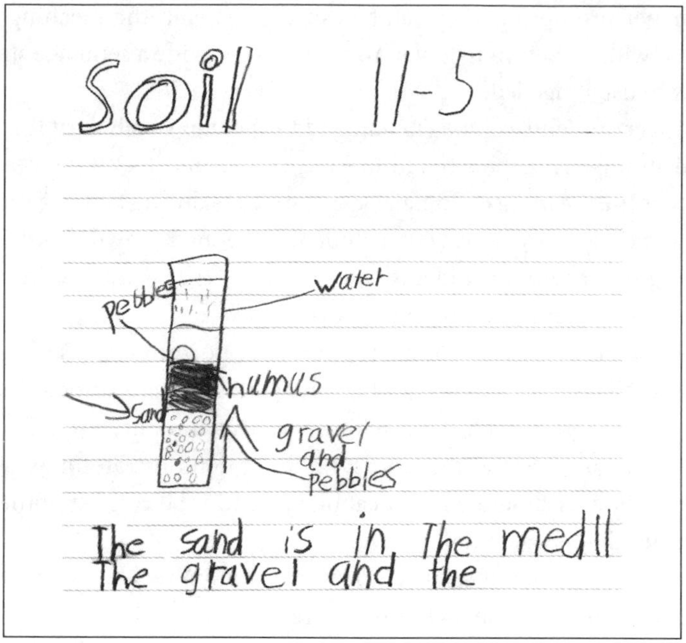

Figure 6–3. A first-grade student uses vocabulary as part of her labeled diagram.

and forms of reading, writing, and speaking in science explicit," according to DiGisi (as cited in Bybee 2002, 41). When used to their full potential, science notebooks help promote the idea that science is a context for literacy development.

THINKING POINT: What role will science notebooks play in literacy development within your classroom?

■   ■   ■

The following chart lists the College and Career Readiness Anchor Standards from the CCSS for ELA (NGA Center & CCSSO 2010) that align with the science notebook. Some connections to these standards might be made during science time, and other connections might be made during a literacy lesson. For example, students might write an argument to support claims related to erosion and deposition.

Strands	Anchor Standards from Common Core State Standards for English Language Arts & Literacy in History/Social Studies, Science, and Technical Subjects K–5
Reading	**1.** Read closely to determine what the text says explicitly and to make logical inferences from it; cite specific textual evidence when writing or speaking to support conclusions drawn from the text.
Writing	**1.** Write arguments to support claims in an analysis of substantive topics or texts, using valid reasoning and relevant and sufficient evidence. **2.** Write informative/explanatory texts to examine and convey complex ideas and information clearly and accurately through the effective selection, organization, and analysis of content. **3.** Write narratives to develop real or imagined experiences or events using effective technique, well-chosen details, and well-structured event sequences. **7.** Conduct short as well as more sustained research projects based on focused questions, demonstrating understanding of the subject under investigation. **8.** Gather relevant information from multiple print and digital sources, assess the credibility and accuracy of each source, and integrate the information while avoiding plagiarism. **9.** Draw evidence from literary or informational texts to support analysis, reflection, and research. **10.** Write routinely over extended time frames (time for research, reflection, and revision) and shorter time frames (a single sitting or a day or two) for a range of tasks, purposes, and audiences.
Speaking and Listening	**1.** Prepare for and participate effectively in a range of conversations and collaborations with diverse partners, building on others' ideas and expressing their own clearly and persuasively. **2.** Integrate and evaluate information presented in diverse media and formats, including visually, quantitatively, and orally. **3.** Evaluate a speaker's point of view, reasoning, and use of evidence and rhetoric. **4.** Present information, findings, and supporting evidence such that listeners can follow the line of reasoning and the organization, development, and style are appropriate to task, purpose, and audience. **5.** Make strategic use of digital media and visual displays of data to express information and enhance understanding of presentations. **6.** Adapt speech to a variety of contexts and communicative tasks, demonstrating command of formal English when indicated or appropriate.
Language Use	**6.** Acquire and use accurately a range of general academic and domain-specific words and phrases sufficient for reading, writing, speaking, and listening at the college and career readiness level.

Bibliography

Achieve, Inc. 2013. *The Next Generation Science Standards.* Washington, DC: National Academies Press. Available at www.nextgenscience.org/. Accessed September 6, 2013.

Belasco, David. 2013. E-mail message to Brian Campbell, September 11.

Bell, Phillip, Leah Bricker, Carrie Tzou, Tiffany Lee, and Katie Van Horne. 2012. "Exploring the Science Framework: Engaging Learners in Scientific Practices Related to Obtaining, Evaluating, and Communicating Information." *Science and Children* 50 (3): 11–16.

Bybee, Rodger W. 2002. *Learning Science and the Science of Learning.* Arlington, VA: NSTA Press.

Duke, Nell. K. 2010. "The Real-World Reading and Writing U.S. Children Need." *Phi Delta Kappan* 91 (5): 68–71.

Duke, Nell. K., Victoria Purcell-Gates, Leigh A. Hall, and Cathy Tower. 2006. "Authentic Literacy Activities for Developing Comprehension and Writing." *The Reading Teacher* 60 (4): 344–55.

Duschl, Richard A. 2012. "The Second Dimension—Crosscutting Concepts." *Science and Children* 49 (6): 10–14.

Dyasi, Rebecca. 2002. Conversation with authors, Las Vegas, NV, 13 June.

Fullerton, Olive. 1995. "Using Talk to Help Learn Mathematics." *English Quarterly* 27 (4): 10–16.

Fulwiler, Betsy R. 2007. *Writing in Science: How to Scaffold Instruction to Support Learning.* Portsmouth, NH: Heinemann.

———. 2011. *Writing in Science in Action.* Portsmouth, NH: Heinemann.

Gallaspy, Alan. 2002. Interview by Brian Campbell and Lori Fulton. Tape recording, Las Vegas, NV, 14 September.

Keys, Carolyn W. 1999. "Revitalizing Instruction in Scientific Genres: Connecting Knowledge Production with Writing to Learn in Science." *Science Education* 83 (2): 115–30.

Lee, Okhee, Helen Quinn, and Guadalupe Valdés. 2013. "Science and Language for English Language Learners in Relation to Next Generation Science Standards and with Implications for Common Core State Standards for English Language Arts and Mathematics." *Educational Researcher* 42 (4): 223–33.

Magbag, Gilbert. 2013. E-mail message to Brian Campbell, 19 August.

Moline, Steve. 1995. *I See What You Mean: Children at Work with Visual Information*. York, ME: Stenhouse.

National Governors Association Center for Best Practices, Council of Chief State School Officers. 2010. *Common Core State Standards for English Language Arts & Literacy in History/Social Studies, Science, and Technical Subjects*. Available at www .corestandards.org. Accessed April 2, 2012.

National Research Council (NRC). 1996. *National Science Education Standards*. Washington, DC: National Academy Press.

———. 2001. *Classroom Assessment and the National Science Education Standards*. Washington, DC: National Academy Press.

———. 2007. *Taking Science to School: Learning and Teaching Science in Grades K–8*. Washington, DC: National Academies Press.

———. 2012. *A Framework for K–12 Science Education: Practices, Crosscutting Concepts, and Core Ideas*. Washington, DC: National Academies Press

Northen, Trent. 2013. Interview by Brian Campbell. Tape recording. Walnut Creek, CA, 14 May.

Norton-Meier, Lori, Brian Hand, Lynn Hockenberry, and Kim Wise. 2008. *Questions, Claims & Evidence: The Important Place of Argument in Children's Science Writing*. Portsmouth, NH: Heinemann.

Reeves, Douglas B. 2000. Teaching and Learning in the Clark County: Keys to Successful Student Achievement (handout). Center for Performance Assessment, Denver, Colorado.

Rivard, Leonard P. 1994. "A Review of Writing to Learn in Science: Implications for Practice and Research." *Journal of Research in Science Teaching* 31 (9): 969–83.

Rohde, Kay. 2002. Interview by Brian Campbell and Lori Fulton. Tape recording. Las Vegas, NV, 5 October.

Ruiz-Primo, Maria. A., Min Li, Shin-Ping Tsai, and Julie Schneider. 2010. "Testing One Premise of Scientific Inquiry in Science Classrooms: Examining Students' Scientific Explanations and Student Learning." *Journal of Research in Science Teaching* 47 (5): 583–608.

Shavelson, Richard J., Yue Yin, Erin M. Furtak, Maria A. Ruiz-Primo, Carlos C. Ayala, Donald B. Young, Miki K. Tomita, Paul R. Brandon, and Francis M. Pottenger III. 2008. "On the Role and Impact of Formative Assessment on Science

Inquiry Teaching and Learning." In *Assessing Science Learning: Perspectives from Research and Practice*, edited by Janet Coffey, Rowena Douglas, and Carole Stearns, 21–36. Arlington, VA: NSTA Press.

Wiliam, Dylan. 2011. *Embedded Formative Assessment.* Bloomington, IN: Solution Tree Press.

Yore, Larry D., Gay L. Bisanz, and Brian M. Hand. 2003. "Examining the Literacy Component of Science Literacy: 25 Years of Language Arts and Science Research." *International Journal of Science Education* 25 (6): 689–725.

Yore, Larry D., Marilyn K. Florence, Terry W. Pearson, and Andrew J. Weaver. 2006. "Written Discourse in Scientific Communities: A Conversation with Two Scientists About Their Views of Science, Use of Language, Role of Writing in Doing Science, and Compatibility Between Their Epistemic Views and Language." *International Journal of Science Education* 28 (2–3): 109–41.

Zembal-Saul, Carla L., Katherine L. McNeill, and Kimber Hershberger. 2013. *What's Your Evidence? Engaging K–5 Students in Constructing Explanations in Science.* Boston: Pearson.